THE CHOICE

Should the Church Affirm
LGBTQ+ Identities and
Ways of Living?

Ron Highfield

Keledei
PUBLICATIONS

An Imprint of Sulis International Press
Los Angeles | Dallas | London

THE CHOICE: SHOULD THE CHURCH AFFIRM LGBTQ+
IDENTITIES AND WAYS OF LIVING?
Copyright ©2024 by Ron Highfield. All rights reserved.

ISBN (print): 978-1-958139-43-1
ISBN (eBook): 978-1-958139-44-8

Published by Keledei Publications
An Imprint of Sulis International
Los Angeles | Dallas | London

www.sulisinternational.com

Contents

The Choice: Introduction

"Are you crazy?" "Are you ready for what's coming?" "Do you *really* want to do this?" Such questions kept circling around in my mind as I considered writing this book.[1] Writing in defense of the traditional view of sex and marriage in today's culture is like trying to swim up Niagara Falls. You're in for a pounding! The dominant culture is so hostile to the biblical way of thinking about sex that it refuses to listen even to the most rational defenses of the biblical view. The moment you voice the slightest qualm about LGBTQ+ ways of living,[2] you are not only dismissed as benighted but attacked as vile. And the assault is often accompanied by weeping and outrage to the point you fear for your safety. This hostile spirit is not limited to X (formerly Twit-

---

[1]Much of the material contained in this book appeared first in my blog [ifaqtheology.com] during the fall of 2021.

[2]It has become the practice of late to use the acronym LGBTQ+ as a catchall term for an indefinite and growing list of so-called "sexual minorities." In this book, I focus on gay men and lesbian women, that is on same-sex relationships. I do not deal with transgender questions. Instead of speaking of "gay and lesbian" people, I will follow a common practice of speaking of "gay people" as an inclusive term.

ter) trolls, progressive legislators, Hollywood actors, and MSNBC commentators. I feel its presence in my workplace, my classroom, and even my church fellowship. The younger generation is either "all in" in affirming LGBTQ+ identities and ways of living, or they are confused, or, if they hold a traditional viewpoint, are intimidated into silence. All around me, voices confidently proclaim that we are not only permitted but obligated to affirm LGBTQ+ identities and ways of living. And the Bible tells us so!

I did not want to write on LGBTQ+ issues because I did not want to get involved in the culture wars with secular people. They accept neither the authority of the Bible nor the consensus of the church's tradition. Nor did I have anything to say to progressive churches, which acknowledge the authority of the Bible only where it fits into progressive culture. But about 10 years ago, I became aware that something had changed. Before that time, I thought Bible-believing Christians, evangelicals, and other conservative believers were united in defending traditional views of sex and marriage against progressive Christians and secular humanists. However, within the past few years, a significant number of highly visible pastors, professors, authors, and church leaders who claimed to be evangelical, Bible-believing, and orthodox urged the church to accept same-sex marriage alongside traditional marriage. Nothing symbolized this change for me more than the 2014 publication of *Changing Our Mind: A Call from America's Leading Evangelical Ethics Scholar for Full Acceptance of LGBTQ Christians in the Church* by

David P. Gushee.[3] Since 2014, the number of books advocating the biblical acceptability of LGBTQ+ ways of living has grown exponentially.[4]

No Alternative

Secular people follow the desires of their hearts without reference to divine law; no surprise there. Nor is it shocking to discover that progressive Christians rationalize their capitulation to progressive culture. But I was taken aback by the claim that you can remain a faithful, Jesus-following, Bible-respecting, Nicene Creed-affirming church while also embracing LGBTQ+ identities and ways of living. I am writing this book to refute this claim. It contradicts biblical morality and distorts the whole biblical faith. Biblical faithfulness and affirmation of LGBTQ+ identities and ways of living aren't compatible and cannot long coexist in the

---

[3]Canton, MI: Read the Spirit Books. *Changing our Mind* is now in its third edition with a new title: *Changing Our Mind: Definitive 3rd Edition of the Landmark Call for Inclusion of LGBTQ Christians with Response to Critics* (2017).

[4]James V. Brownson, *Bible, Gender, Sexuality: Reframing the Church's Debate on Same-Sex Relationships* (Grand Rapids: Eerdmans, 2013) is the most sophisticated and effective advocate I have read. I've read many less scholarly works advocating the same thesis and using the same arguments, among which are: Colby Martin, *Unclobber: Rethinking our Misuse of the Bible on Homosexuality* (Louisville: Westminster John Knox, 2016); Matthew Vines, *God and the Gay Christian* (New York: Convergent Books, 2014); and Brandan J. Robertson, *The Gospel of Inclusion: A Christian Case for LGBT+ Inclusion in the Church* (Eugene, OR: Cascade Books, 2022).

same mind. When mixed together they form an unstable blend that will eventually resolve into its constituents. Evangelical churches and individuals that affirm LGBTQ+ ways of living will eventually become progressive or return to their biblical roots.[5] More likely, such churches will divide into warring parties that will eventually go their separate ways.[6] I did not write this book to give practical advice to the church about its pastoral and evangelistic ministries to LGBTQ+ people. These important tasks should not be neglected. But other authors possess more experience than I in these areas. I am writing, rather, about the fundamental doctrine that must guide all such ministries. If the church gets doctrine wrong, practical wrongs are sure to follow. Not only so, other erroneous doctrines will inevitably exert their logical force and practical demands. Nor am I speaking solely about the church's message to people living today. I am speaking about the church's solemn duty to preserve the whole truth of Christianity for generations yet unborn.

Many others, too, have written in defense of the traditional view of sex and marriage. In an older book that

---

[5]This separation is already on full display in the career of David P. Gushee. In 2014, he presented himself as "America's leading evangelical ethics scholar." In his 2020 book, *After Evangelicalism: The Path to a New Christianity* (Louisville: Westminster John Knox), he separates himself from evangelicalism.
[6]See Roger Olson, *Against Liberal Theology: Putting the Brakes on Progressive Christianity* (Grand Rapids: Zondervan, 2022). Olson argues that evangelical churches that adopt progressive elements such as LGBTQ+ affirmation will find it almost impossible to resist moving into full-fledged Liberal Christianity, which is not Christianity at all.

still merits close study, Robert A. J. Gagnon, *The Bible and Homosexual Practice: Texts and Hermeneutics,* presents an exhaustive study of all the biblical texts relevant to the issue of same-sex practice.[7] In another big, scholarly book just published, Rubel Shelly, *Male & Female God Made Them: A Biblical Review of LGBTQ+ Claims,* places the debate about interpretation of the biblical references to same-sex activity within the larger context of the biblical view of creation, sex, and marriage.[8] Many other fine books take up this cause at a popular level. So why should I write another? I have written about the doctrine of God, creation, providence, atonement, apologetics, women's ordination, and the church. Now we find ourselves confronted with what I believe will be a defining issue of our time: will the church of Christ abandon the biblical view of what it means to be a human being and adopt a subjective view of human nature and identity? Should the church accept an individual's self-identification as gay, lesbian, bisexual, queer, or transgender as replacements for the biblical identities of male and female, child of God, and image of God? Should the church go even further and adopt transhumanism, wherein a person possesses no given nature and retains only their subjective identity as "me"? Given what is at stake, how can I remain silent?

---

[7]Nashville: Abington, 2002.

[8]Joplin, MO: College Press, 2023. See also Shelly's popular work on the subject: *The Ink is Dry: God's Distinctive Word on Marriage, Family, and Sexual Responsibility* (Joplin, MO: College Press, 2023). See also Jeffrey Peterson, "The Nuptial Vision of the Bible and its Opponents," *Journal of Christian Studies,* 1/2 (May 2022): 9-31.

Of what value is a theologian who cowers in silence in the hour of greatest need on the very issue that most needs to be addressed? Though I did not want to speak about the LGBTQ+ issue, I believe I have no alternative.

Is it, then, for conscience's sake alone that I speak? What do I have to offer that other authors do not? Having read many fine books in defense of the biblical view, I still think I can contribute to this debate. First, I intend to avoid a rhetorical trap into which many defenders of the tradition fall, that is, accepting an equal or greater burden of proof than advocates of change are willing to bear. Proponents of LGBTQ+ affirmation seek to establish the affirming position as a legitimate alternative to the traditional view. We must, they contend, reexamine the scriptures without prejudice. That is to say, we should not presume the traditional view true and burden the affirming view with the task of overcoming this presumption. Instead, those advocating the traditional view must show why it is to be preferred. If its defenders cannot demonstrate its superiority, the traditional view loses its status as the only legitimate position. The affirming view attains legitimacy as a living option. I reject this reversal and am determined to hold affirming authors to the burden of proof. Because the Bible and the church have spoken with one voice for 3,200 years in condemning same-sex intercourse, the church has earned the right to demand advocates of change bear a heavy burden of proof. Indeed, it has a duty to do so.

Second, I believe I can contribute to this discussion by employing a rigorous analytic approach to the subject. Arguments presented by advocates of LGBTQ+ affirmation are often subtle and speculative. You have to read them many times to see their force and find their fallacies. At strategic points, they appeal to emotions and values embedded in progressive culture. I believe that I have developed the analytical and critical skills needed to see through their rhetorical strategies. Moreover, I've developed some immunity to emotional manipulation.

My Method

But how to proceed? I didn't want to write a comprehensive survey of the literature on this subject. The question I want to answer for my readers is not what has been said, but what must be proved in order to demonstrate the "affirming" position.[9] I am writing to individuals and churches that want to be true to the Bible's teaching on faith, practice, and morality. I aim to help them understand and reject the argument that they can both affirm LGBTQ+ identities and ways of living and remain faithful to the Bible's teaching. I believe I can best accomplish this goal by describing, ana-

---

[9] I reluctantly use the term "affirming" to refer to the viewpoint that the church should accept LGBTQ+ identities and ways of living as morally equivalent to traditional marriage between male and female. Most often, opponents of the traditional position designate it as "non-affirming." These terms obviously bias the discussion in favor of the "affirming" stance.

lyzing and critiquing one representative book that makes a persuasive case for the "affirming" position. I chose Karen Keen, *Scripture, Ethics, and the Possibility of Same-Sex Relationships* to play this role.[10] Why this book? Though Keen is not an elite biblical scholar, historian, or theologian, she is a well-educated person. She holds a Master of Theology degree from Duke Divinity School and has done further graduate work in Judaism and Christianity in Antiquity at Marquette University. She is Director of the Redwood Center for Spiritual Care & Education.[11] Her book is short and written in a popular style. But some may ask, "why not examine the most scholarly book advocating the thesis you want to examine?"[12] My reasons are simple: books written in an academic style make arguments based on knowledge of ancient languages and cultures. They construct elaborate arguments from church history, psychology, sociology, and biology. Because the average person cannot assess the soundness of such elite arguments, they are tempted to trust whichever expert makes the case for the conclusion they favor.

---

[10]Grand Rapids: Eerdmans, 2018. I will place page references to Keen's book within the text enclosed in parentheses. I will supplement Keen's arguments at certain points with references to other authors, mostly in footnotes. For the most part, I will stay focused on her argument. I have read enough in this literature to be confident that I have heard the best arguments that can be made supporting the affirming position.

[11]https://www.redwoodspiritualcare.com/

[12]For example, James V. Brownson, *Bible, Gender, Sexuality: Reframing the Church's Debate on Same-Sex Relationships* (Grand Rapids: Eerdmans, 2013). Brownson's book is three times as long as Keen's book.

I consider the brevity and popular style of Keen's book an advantage in speaking to the audience I want to reach. In fact, we are writing to the same audience, that is, Christian believers who view the Bible as the definitive authority for faith, religious practice, and morals. She defends one of the most conservative positions available among advocates of LGBTQ+ affirmation. As far as I can tell, she does not approve of polyamory or give up the ideal of life-long faithfulness to one partner. She merely brings same-sex marriages under the same set of rules as traditional marriages. Her conservative viewpoint may appeal to believers open to accepting gay relationships, but who would take offense at advocates of polyamory and promiscuity.[13] Indeed, hers is the most persuasive book I've read written to an evangelical audience, and that alone makes it worthy of close examination. She argues in a simple way that can be evaluated by ordinary Christians based on their knowledge of English translations of the Bible, common-sense principles of interpretation, and moral reasoning open to all. Yet, Keen has incorporated material from elite biblical, historical, and theological works. Hence, I am confident that by analyzing and critiquing her work, I am also evaluating the most persuasive arguments of elite scholars.

---

[13]As I will explain as the book unfolds, I do not believe Keen's "conservative" position is tenable. Its implications are much more radical than she admits or perhaps than she knows. In any case, I consider the position she defends as a sugar-coated poison pill.

I will follow Keen's argument in the order she develops it. My presentation will include description, analysis and critique of her arguments. I will do my best to describe her views fairly. I am mindful that most readers of my book will not have read Keen's book. Accordingly, I will summarize the essential message of each chapter for the reader. In analysis, I will break her arguments down into their components to show how she moves from premises to conclusions. In my critique, I will evaluate the validity, truth, and persuasive power of her reasoning by criteria that I share with her and my target audience.

Part I. The Argument for Gay-Affirming Evangelical Christianity

In Part I, consisting of eleven chapters, I will unfold Karen Keen's argument for gay-affirming evangelical theology step by step with its supporting evidence and rebuttals of opposing arguments. Along the way, I will analyze her arguments into their component parts so that readers can see clearly the flow of her logic and apply their own critical reasoning to her conclusions. My critical comments will focus on her central contention that affirming covenanted gay relationships as morally equivalent to traditional marriage between one man and one woman is compatible with the traditional evangelical view of biblical authority. I will argue that Keen fails to demonstrate this thesis; indeed, it is false.

1. The Plan

In this chapter, I will lay out the essential argument of Keen's book so we can begin our micro analysis with the big picture in mind. The overall argument can be stated as a short series of assertions followed by a conclusion. Assertions one through three are principles of biblical interpretation, and assertions four through six are derived from the experience of gay people as described in their self-testimony. The conclusion follows from combining assertions one through six.

Interpretive Principle #1
The Bible's positive moral teachings provide a vision of justice, goodness, and peace; they are intended to promote human flourishing.

Interpretive Principle #2
The Bible's moral prohibitions are intended to forbid things that cause harm to human beings and the rest of creation.

Interpretive Principle #3
To apply the Bible's moral teachings appropriately, we must deliberate about whether or not applying a biblical rule to a situation prevents harm and promotes human flourishing. Applications that harm people must be rejected.

Experienced-based Fact #1
Gay people do not choose to be gay, and the overwhelming majority cannot change their orientation.

Experienced-based Fact #2
Faithful, loving gay relationships do not cause harm to those involved or to the human community. To the contrary, they can display all the fruits of the Spirit listed in Scripture.

Experienced-based Fact #3
A large majority of gay people do not have the gift of celibacy and find that state deeply painful.

Conclusion
Because covenanted same-sex relationships embody justice, goodness, and human flourishing, do not cause harm to the people in the relationship or the human community, and unwanted celibacy causes great unhappiness to gay people, faithful deliberation must conclude that the Bible allows covenanted same-sex relationships.

In her book, Keen develops this seven-part argument in detail. We must follow her reasoning from beginning to end to grasp the full import of her case. However, even at this early stage we can see where she is headed. Her argument for accepting same-sex relationships is completely hopeless if interpreting the Bible's moral teaching is simply a matter of getting clear on its specific commands. For the Bible specifically condemns same-sex intercourse in the most severe terms and encourages faithful marriage only between male and female. Hence Keen's first three principles outline an interpretive strategy that focuses on the motivations behind the Bible's commands and on the general principles they embody rather than on the rules themselves. According to Keen, discerning God's will involves more than merely understanding what the Bible commands. We are obligated to obey specific biblical commands only insofar as we can see that they embody justice and goodness and promote human flourishing in our circumstances.

Perhaps to some readers Keen's three principles of biblical interpretation sound innocent enough. But further thought shows that they imply a dramatic revolution in the way the church uses the Bible in its moral teaching. In fact, her principles deprive every specific biblical command of its authority as written. Biblical commands no longer transparently reveal God's will. This interpretive strategy defeats in one sweeping move every simple appeal to biblical commands as grounds for the church's moral teaching.[14] As is clear from her use of experience-based facts, her interpretive model opens a huge field for private experience and psychosocial theory to have a decisive say in what we judge to be good or harmful. Since we know that God wants only justice and human flourishing, we can now replace every biblical command we judge counterproductive to these aspirations with a human judgment about what is happiness-producing in our situation.

---

[14]Keen's strategy adumbrated here is typical of affirming writers. Brownson, *Bible, Gender, Sexuality,* for example, speaks of the necessity of interpreting specific texts in light of the Bible's "underlying moral logic." On almost every page, Brownson reminds us to ask *why* a text forbids this or that behavior. For example: "But noting the vehemence or intensity of the text does not yet identify its underlying moral logic. Paul may be speaking intensely here [Romans 1], but in observing that[,] we have not yet discerned *why* the same-sex relations he depicts are to be understood as wrong" (p. 17).

2. The Narrative

In her first chapter ("The Church's Response to the Gay and Lesbian Community: A Brief History"), Keen sets the stage for her biblical argument by telling the story of the ancient and modern church's response to the practice of same-sex intercourse.[15] Traditional thinkers take the church's universal condemnation of homosexual practice as evidence in favor of traditional interpretations of Scripture. Keen repurposes this narrative by presenting it as a history of misunderstanding, hatred, and ignorance. She tells this story in a way sure to offend modern sensibilities, which have been shaped by the narrative of oppression and liberation that structures the contemporary mind's interpretation of history.

---

[15]For the most part, I will adopt Keen's practice of speaking of people as "gay" or "lesbian," though I think using these terms begs the important question of the nature of sexual "orientation." Moreover, using the terms "gay" and "lesbian" is anachronistic when speaking of pre-modern understandings of same-sex intercourse.

People

The first line of the chapter captures its message in one sentence: "When it comes to same-sex relationships, there is one thing we cannot forget: *people*" (p. 1). Gays are real people. In this chapter, Keen aims to expose the ways the church has dehumanized gay people and advance the process of re-humanizing them. According to Keen, the church's lack of understanding of gay people clouds its ability to make good judgments about the Christian legitimacy of same-sex relationships. Correcting the caricatures of gay people is the first step toward reading the Bible with an open mind. John Chrysostom (347-407) called same-sex intercourse a "monstrous insanity." Martin Luther argued that same-sex desire originates from the perverting influence of the devil. Matthew Henry asserts that such desires are divine punishments consequent on a prior abandonment of God. Pre-modern medical explanations for same-sex desire usually picture gay people as mentally ill or suffering from disease. Keen could have expanded this section indefinitely, but these few examples serve to represent the church's dominant premodern attitude.

Keen next surveys five stances that have characterized conservative churches over the past sixty years. Although Keen views these differing approaches as ordered chronologically, she also recognizes that they exist simultaneously at the present time. I will simply list them in order in Keen's own words:

1. "Gay people should stay in the closet" (p. 4).

2. "Gay people are perverts and criminals" (p. 4).

3. "Gay people are hapless victims who need healing" (p. 6).

4. "Gay people are admirable saints called to a celibate life" (p. 9).

5. "Gay people are…." (p. 11).

Under heading 5, Keen attempts to picture the landscape at the time of her writing. She describes four group stances: celibate gays, ex-gays, same-sex attracted evangelicals who deny the reality of same-sex "orientations," and gay affirming evangelicals. Although she writes about these four stances in a descriptive style, she clearly favors the "affirming" position. Stances 1-4 do not meet the divine intention test because they do not promote justice, goodness, and human flourishing. The thesis of her book, after all, is that evangelical churches may adopt the "affirming" position as biblically sound.

Analysis

It might seem that this chapter ("A Brief History") simply sets the stage for the book's argument by documenting the history of the subject and surveying contemporary options. However, I want to suggest three ways in which the chapter argues against the traditional view and for the affirming view. First, Keen's description of how premodern authors speak about gay people makes a subtle argument. Keen clearly expects the contemporary reader to cringe upon hearing gay people described with such terms. Figures of the past who expressed disgust and hatred toward groups with whom contemporary society has become sympathetic lose credibility with modern audiences; they are made toxic by being labeled racist, sexist, or homophobic. Given contemporary society's sympathies, rational and biblical arguments critical of gay people fall on deaf ears because of suspicion that they are rationalizations for irrational animus. Keen employs here a postmodern variation of the genetic fallacy, which uses speculations about authors' motives to cast doubt on their conclusions. Second, rehearsing traditionalists' dubious arguments and implausible speculations about the origins of same-sex desire leaves the impression that the conclusions traditionalists draw about biblical morality must also be false or at least doubtful. Weak arguments can undermine even the strongest case.

Third, Keen urges us to cease thinking of issues in abstraction from *people*. Gay people are individuals with feelings, experiences, and stories. In doing this she not only draws on society's sympathy for gay people, but prepares readers to accept the self-reported experiences of gay people as proof of three important assertions within her master argument: (1) people do not choose to become gay, (2) they cannot change their orientation, and (3) maintaining a life of celibacy is very painful. Accordingly, Keen speculates that "if historical trends continue, whatever paradigm shifts occur in the future will likely flow from gay and lesbian Christians truthfully testifying about their lived reality" (p. 14).

Danger Zone

Before I offer my critique, I want to address a huge obstacle that makes effective criticism of Keen's book almost impossible: her book is autobiography as well as argument. It concerns personal identity, feelings, and experience as well as thought, history, and biblical interpretation. It is only with great difficulty that modern audiences can separate these two dimensions. The overarching narrative tells a compelling story of oppression, suffering, agony and suicide on the one hand, and courage, determination and endurance on the other. Indeed, the persuasive power of the book lies in its brilliant combination of autobiography and rational argument. Because these two features are woven together in a seamless whole, critique of its rational aspects will be taken as critique of the personal elements as well, as a poisonous attack on the person making the argument. Telling other people what they feel, dismissing their sense of identity or denying their self-reported experiences appears to most contemporary people as profoundly insensitive. From the postmodern perspective, autobiography is argument.

What is the critic to do? Some authors rush blindly into this rhetorical trap, blurting out the stupidest things. Needless to say, no matter how clever their arguments, they lose the audience the minute they open their mouths! Others see the trap, realize that their situation is untenable and decide not to say anything. Their silence allows weak arguments to take cover under a strong narrative. Lack of objection will be taken as acquiescence. My strategy will be to keep the reader aware of Keen's narrative appeals to compassion and other feelings as I examine her arguments from a rational and biblical perspective.

Critique

It is too early to develop a comprehensive critique of the three arguments implicit in this chapter, because in the following chapters she expands them extensively. Additionally, the book constitutes one big argument; it needs to be assessed as a whole. However, I will venture some preliminary observations on these three arguments.

Regarding #1: This argument relies on the rhetorical advantage gay people have acquired over the past few decades. For a variety of reasons, including the HIV/AIDS crisis of the late twentieth century, a sympathetic media and decisions by the Supreme Court of the United States, there has developed a social consensus that gay people have been innocent victims of prejudice and violence. This consensus narrative places an unwarrantedly heavy burden of proof on those who argue the traditional thesis from the Bible.[16] For there is no logical connection between the cringeworthy way in which traditionalists of the past spoke about same-sex activity and the truth of their conclusions about biblical teaching on this subject.

Regarding #2: Discovering that many arguments offered to support a thesis are weak or less than demonstrative does not prove that the thesis is false. For sure, rehearsing a litany of the weakest arguments in support of a conclusion tends to create doubt in the listener. However, the mere possibility of doubt does not justify rejecting a thesis as false.

Regarding #3: Indeed, gay people are *people.* I agree that we ought to treat gay people as human beings worthy of respect. However, this is true of every person we meet. There is no connection between remembering that an individual is worthy of respect and affirming everything they do as morally upright or accepting their self-described experience as evidence for the "affirming" thesis. Though it would be ridiculous to deny that a person feels what they say they feel, we are under no obligation to accept a person's subjective feelings as proof for what is objectively right. Making this inference into a general rule would result in moral anarchy.

---

[16]This shift in who bears the burden of proof affects profoundly the openness (or lack of it) of contemporary audiences to the traditional view. Which party bears the burden of proof is not a logical issue but a rhetorical one. It depends on the expectations of the audience you wish to persuade. Many if not most contemporary audiences come to the table intolerant of any criticisms of LGBTQ+ identities and ways of living.

3. Between the Lines

In chapter 2, Keen surveys "Same-Sex Relations in Ancient Jewish and Christian Thought." She documents the universally negative view of same-sex relationships in the Old and New Testaments and in such Jewish writers as Philo and Josephus. Although she delays detailed examination of the biblical texts that refer to same-sex intercourse, she briefly mentions two Old Testament texts (Leviticus 18:22 and 20:13) and three New Testament texts (Romans 1:18-32; 1 Corinthians 6:9-10; and 1 Timothy 1:9-10). She admits that these texts condemn same-sex relationships. Progressives, traditionalists, and Keen agree on this point. But this consensus does not settle the hermeneutical issue, that is, how to interpret these texts. For even traditionalists admit that there are many biblical commands—for example, about modest dress, gender specific clothing, not eating blood—that we are free to set aside because they address circumstances that no longer exist or they were originally given for reasons that are culture-bound.

According to Keen, to decide whether or not biblical prohibitions against same-sex relationships are universally binding we must ask *what kind of* same-sex relationships the biblical authors had in mind and *why* they condemned them. In her survey of biblical texts, she proposes five discernible reasons why the Bible may have condemned same-sex relationships:

1. "Violation of gender norms" (p. 19); that is, culturally relative boundaries and rules for relations between the sexes.

2. "Lack of procreative potential" (p. 19). This objection assumes that openness to the possibility of procreation is an essential component of marriage.

3. "Participation in pagan practice" (p. 19).

4. "Participation in common or religious prostitution" (p. 19).

5. "Unrestrained or excessive lust" (p. 19).

Concerning the question of what kind of same-sex relationships the biblical authors had in mind when issuing their condemnations, Keen relies on the "progressive" argument that the biblical authors denounce practices that involved "exploitation and misogynistic gender norms" rather than loving, covenanted same-sex relationships.[17] Hence, we should not without due hermeneutical reflection apply these texts to practices not in view when originally written. I find it interesting that Keen does not say whether or not she agrees with this "progressive" strategy, even though it becomes apparent in succeeding chapters that it plays a vital role in her argument. She is very careful here to protect her evangelical credentials from being tainted by association with progressivism, Christian or secular.[18] Maintaining rapport with her target audience depends on it.

---

[17]As an example of a progressive writer arguing this case, see Robert K. Gnuse, "Seven Gay Texts: Biblical Passages Used to Condemn Homosexuality" *(Biblical Theology Bulletin* 45. 2 [2015]: 68-87). Gnuse concludes, "I believe that there is no passage in the biblical text that **truly** condemns a sexual relationship between two adult, free people, who truly love each other….[Hence] biblical texts should not be called forth in the condemnation of gay and lesbian people in our society" (p. 83). I will examine Gnuse's interpretive strategy in Part II of this book.

[18]Matthew Vines, in *God and the Gay Christian,* is another relative conservative advocate of gay affirmation who uses progressive interpretations but distances himself from the progressive view of the Bible: "To be fair," Vines explains, "many Christians now support same-sex relationships. But a number of those who do tend to see Scripture as a helpful but dated guidebook, not as the final authority on questions of morality and doctrine….That is not my view of Scripture…I believe all Scripture is inspired by God and authoritative for my life" (p. 2).

Analysis

Like chapter one of Keen's book, this chapter is more than mere description. It makes an argument and sets the agenda for the book's further arguments. In her description of ancient views of same-sex relationships, she acknowledges that the Bible condemns same-sex intercourse, and ironically this admission is the beginning gambit of her argument for their legitimacy. First, by granting the Bible's prohibition of same-sex intercourse without conceding her overall case, she neutralizes one of the traditionalist's best arguments, that is, the seemingly obvious assumption that the Bible's repeated condemnation of same-sex intercourse applies to any form of such intercourse. *Why* people engage in same-sex intercourse is completely irrelevant. For the traditionalist, the absence of concern about the motivations for same-sex relationships within the Bible speaks volumes about how it views them. If anything, the Bible assumes that the motives for engaging in same-sex acts must be corrupt because the act itself is corrupt. Anyone arguing otherwise bears a huge burden of proof.

In a second astute move, Keen asserts without argument that the reasons (or intentions or motives) for a biblical author's condemnation of same-sex intercourse determine the legitimacy and scope of the prohibition. Hence if we become convinced that the reasons for the condemnation were misinformed, based on shifting cultural norms, prejudiced or arising from ignorance, we may reject or correct them. If none of these reasons can be convincingly shown to be applicable to *all* same-sex relationships, then the universal scope of such commands is placed in doubt. Notice how Keen shifts the burden of proof from those who affirm that some types of same-sex relationships are permissible to those who condemn all of them. Something that had been obvious—that the Bible condemns same-sex intercourse—now becomes problematic. Unless the traditionalist can prove the universality of the reasons behind the command, the traditionalist stands defeated and the possibility of biblically approved same-sex relationships becomes plausible.

Third, by establishing the necessity of discovering the underlying reasons for the Bible's prohibitions against gay relationships, Keen has opened the possibility of excluding loving, covenanted same-sex relationships from these biblical prohibitions. If the underlying reasons for the biblical condemnations have to do with the presence of coercion and abuse rather than with the biological sex of the participants, a case can be made that these texts do not condemn loving same-sex relationships.

Critical Remarks

Regarding #1: Keen's gambit of admitting that the Bible condemns same-sex intercourse may not be as effective as she thinks. For her argument will work only if she can compile an exhaustive list of the reasons (or intentions and motives) for biblical prohibitions. Traditionalists could reply they will not allow a hermeneutical strategy based on speculation, silence, and reading between the lines to undermine the plain meaning of the text. That would be a very unevangelical thing to do!

Regarding #2: Keen lists five possible reasons why the Bible condemns same-sex acts. Each of the five reasons, she will argue, can be plausibly dismissed as inapplicable to loving, covenanted same-sex relationships. However, she does not list among the irrelevant biblical reasons the conviction that God created male and female for each other, that is, what she calls "gender complementarity" (p. 20). Including this "reason" would damage her case, because it cannot be easily dismissed as inapplicable to loving same-sex relationships. Whatever speculations we may propose about *why* the Bible condemns same-sex sexual intercourse, we must still ask whether or not a biblical command's legitimacy depends on discovering a rationale for it that makes sense to us. Keen keeps reminding us that she is an evangelical, believes as do all evangelicals in biblical inspiration, and that she seeks God's will in these texts. She wishes to present arguments that evangelicals can accept without giving up their evangelical faith. As an evangelical, shouldn't Keen acknowledge the possibility that God possesses reasons for his commands that are hidden from us?

Regarding #3: Keen adopts an interpretive strategy that allows her to dismiss the specific biblical command against same-sex intercourse because it does not embody the ethical principle she thinks it should have embodied. If followed consistently, this strategy would sweep away all biblical wisdom embodied in the law and even in the teaching and life of Jesus and his apostles in favor of our own sense of what it means to be a loving, just, and faithful person. After all, where do we learn what a Christian understanding of love, justice, and faithfulness is but in the specific commands and examples in the Bible?

4. The Clash

In Chapter 3 ("Key Arguments in Today's Debate on Same-sex Relationships"), Keen sets up a debate between traditionalists and progressives about the biblical view of same-sex relationships.[19] It focuses on the significance of "gender and anatomical complementarity" (p. 25) for the issue. In previous chapters, Keen concluded that traditionalists and progressives agree that the Bible condemns same-sex relationships for a variety of reasons—idolatry, coercion, and exploitation. But they disagree on the crucial issue of whether or not the Bible forbids same-sex relationships because of their lack of "gender and anatomical complementarity." Traditionalists argue that the Bible requires such complementarity for legitimate marriage. Progressives argue that the essence of marriage is "covenant fidelity" (p. 30), not sexual differentiation. The debate turns on the interpretation of six texts: Genesis 1-3; Matthew 19:1-6; Mark 10:1-9; Romans 1:22-28; Ephesians 5:22-32; and Revelation 19:7-9.

---

[19]"Key Arguments in Today's Debate on Same-sex Relationships" (pp. 25-42).

Keen sets out the traditionalist argument against same-sex relationships in four theses and the progressive case in five theses:

Traditionalist Arguments

The Bible teaches that "gender and anatomical complementarity" is an essential feature of legitimate marriage because…

1. "Heterosexual marriage is a creation ordinance, and therefore not culturally relative" (p. 26). [Genesis 1:27; 2:24; Matthew 19:4-6]

2. "Marriage is ordered toward procreation, but procreation is not required to validate marriage" (p. 27). [Genesis 1:28]

3. "Same-sex desire is the result of the fall" (p. 28). [Romans 1:22-28; Genesis 3]

4. "Heterosexual marriage is a living icon or a symbol of the union of Christ and the church" (p. 29). [Ephesians 5:25; 29-32; Revelation 19:7-9]

Traditionalist arguments appeal in a straightforward way to the texts they quote: The Bible obviously prohibits same-sex intercourse and commends marriage as a God-sanctioned covenant, which it never contemplates as anything other than a union of male and female.

Therefore…

The Bible teaches that "gender and anatomical complementarity" is an essential feature of legitimate marriage.

Progressive Counter Arguments

The Bible does **not** teach that "gender and anatomical complementarity" is an essential feature of legitimate marriage because...

1. "Covenant fidelity, not sexual differentiation, is the foundation of biblical marriage" (p. 30).

2. "Procreation is minimized in the New Testament" (p. 33).

3. "Paul's use of "unnatural" *(para physin)* in Romans 1 must be understood in his historical context" (p. 35).

4. "Romans 1 does not describe most gay and lesbian people" (p. 36).

5. "Same-sex relationships can symbolize the union between Christ and the church" (p. 39).[20]

The cumulative force of these progressive theses is mostly negative. They propose exceptions and alternative explanations to the traditional interpretations,

---

[20]No progressive author I've read argues that if Paul were asked whether he would exempt faithful, covenanted same-sex relationships from his condemnations in Romans 1, he would say "yes." But progressives are not bothered by this.

thereby creating doubt about traditionalists' exclusive claims. Newly formed doubt and alternative explanations wedge open the possibility that "gender and anatomical complementarity" may not be an essential feature of legitimate marriage. At this point, affirming same-sex relationships as biblically legitimate is a mere possibility. It needs further support to increase its credibility. Keen offers that support in succeeding chapters.

Analysis

This chapter operates on two levels. Our attention is drawn first to the debate between traditionalists and progressives. Although Keen denies that she fits in either camp, she nevertheless uses a progressive voice to represent the viewpoint she accepts. Why does she do this? Throughout the chapter Keen's invisible hand is at work using this debate for her own purposes. But it is not until the next chapter that she tells us that the debate between traditionalists and progressives ends in a "stalemate" (p. 43). This conclusion opens space for Keen to make her own contribution, which she does in the rest of the book. There may be, however, another reason Keen uses the progressive voice to critique traditionalist arguments. Christian defenses of same-sex relationships have been for the most part articulated by progressives. Rejecting biblical authority, embracing historical relativism, and adhering to theological liberalism give them greater freedom to question even the plain meaning of the Bible and look for alternative interpretations. Keen does not wish to be associated with this aspect of progressivism. However, she uses the imaginative work of progressives to put these alternative interpretations into our minds. It is an open question, however, whether you can justify the conclusions progressives reach without accepting the whole progressive package. Keen argues that you can do so. I argue that you cannot.

Keen devotes nearly three times as much space to progressive arguments as to traditionalist ones. Perhaps this lack of balance makes sense because the traditionalist case is simple whereas the progressive case is complicated. The traditionalist needs only point to biblical texts, which clearly condemn same-sex intercourse and commend marriage between male and female. What more needs to be said? Traditionalists presume that anyone who wishes to challenge the consensus of the church's tradition bears the burden of proof. Progressives, however, must argue against the grain of the plain meaning of the text. Each of the five progressive theses listed above attempts to defeat the traditional reading of the biblical proof texts. The effect of the five progressive arguments is to create doubt and stimulate us to imagine alternative interpretations. I don't think I am being uncharitable to surmise that Keen gives much more space to progressive arguments because she agrees with them and wants to persuade us of their strength while maintaining her distance from progressivism's offensive features—offensive, that is, to conservative, Bible-believing Christians.

Critical Comments

I will make my critical comments brief. I don't want to go into detail in a critique of the chapter's progressive arguments because Keen has not yet tied herself to them or explained just where she agrees and disagrees with them. I do not want to risk attributing to her something she has not affirmed. In any case, my critique of progressivism would begin at a more fundamental level than interpretation of the six texts discussed in this chapter. Tellingly, Keen uses the term "heterosexual marriage" to designate the traditionalist understanding of biblical marriage. Usually, Keen resists using terms that attribute a modern idea to an ancient author. She violates that rule here. Traditionalists should not accept this term as descriptive of what they believe. In the Bible, marriage means just one thing. It needs no qualifier. To add the adjective "heterosexual" begs the essential question, and thoughtful traditionalists will not overlook this fallacy. Keen has not yet clearly differentiated herself from what she calls "progressive" Christian theology. Hence the reader is kept in the dark about her theological stance and is forced to guess what she is up to. Her thesis is that you do not need to reject biblical authority or your evangelical faith to accept same-sex sexual relationships as legitimate. But her use of insights generated on progressive premises and developed using progressive methods evokes some suspicion about her sincerity in claiming to support an evangelical view of biblical authority.

5. Designer Interpretation I

Keen next develops arguments she thinks attain progressive results apart from progressive theology. Because her next two chapters combine to form one argument, I will delay my critique of chapter 4 until I have summarized and analyzed chapter 5.

The Target Audience (Again)

As you think about Keen's argument and my critiques, keep in mind her target audience and the constraints this focus places on her reasoning and my responses. She speaks to evangelicals, to people who wish to remain loyal to the principle of biblical authority. They will not accept the progressive view of the Bible's moral teaching, which dismisses it as primitive, uninformed, and of mere human origin. Though Keen rehearses progressives' arguments and obviously accepts some of their conclusions, she labors to distance herself from their liberal theological presuppositions. Hence to achieve her purpose of steering clear of both extremes, Keen must develop an interpretive strategy that both affirms biblical authority *and* demonstrates that same-sex relationships are morally acceptable. She devotes chapters 4 and 5 to this task. Below I will devote space to summarizing, clarifying, and critiquing the method she develops in these chapters.

A Theory of Interpretation

The title of chapter 4 gives us a feel for what is to come: "Fifty Shekels for Rape: Making Sense of Old Testament Laws." In this chapter, Keen compares two Old Testament case laws found in Exodus 21:22-25 and 28-30 to similar cases found in law codes of other ancient near eastern peoples. In Keen's view, the similarity of Old Testament laws to those of non-Israelite nations demonstrates that they share a common cultural milieu. Progressives take this commonality to prove that such laws are wholly irrelevant to our time, and traditionalists ignore the challenge this discovery poses to their proof text method of biblical interpretation. Keen proposes a theory of interpretation that takes seriously the cultural relativity of biblical laws while preserving their divine authority. To do this, she distinguishes between the culturally conditioned laws and the underlying purposes of those laws. We may view the underlying principles as divinely inspired while viewing specific instructions as culturally conditioned applications of those values. It is a mistake, Keen argues, to focus on *what* the laws instruct the Israelites to do rather than on *why* the laws were given and the goals at which they aim. In a section on the "enduring meaning of Old Testament laws," Keen makes the following assertions:

> Inspiration resides not necessarily in the particularities, but in the overarching reason for the laws—namely a good and just society. (p. 50)

> Sin is generally defined by what harms other. (p. 50)

> Thus, whether and how we apply a particularity from scriptural mandates depends on the underlying intent of the law and its relationship to fostering a good and just world. (p. 51)

> What both progressives and traditionalists typically overlook is the deliberative process that we must undertake to rightly interpret and apply biblical laws today. (p. 51)

The chapter concludes with two questions that prepare the reader for the next phase of the argument:

> What is the overarching intent of the Bible's sexual laws? Are there alternative ways to fulfill that intent more fully that take into consideration the predicament of gay and lesbian people? (pp. 51-52)

Analytic Observation

In constructing her method of interpretation, Keen argues that the specific behaviors biblical laws enjoin or forbid are culturally conditioned applications of such universal and divinely inspired principles as justice, peace, mercy, and love. We are obligated to respect those universal principles everywhere and always, but we are not bound by previous attempts to embody those principles in specific mandates. According to this inter-pretive strategy, we are obligated to honor the Bible's specific rules forbidding same-sex relationships only insofar as those rules embody the universal principles of justice, peace, mercy and love in our contemporary situation. Her success in convincing evangelicals of the biblical permissibility of loving, same-sex relationships depends on demonstrating the universal validity and workability of her hermeneutical principle. Does her method of interpretation help us grasp the unchanging divine meaning of the scriptures as she claims, or does it give us license to find our own values and meanings underneath the words of Scripture? This question poses one of the two or three most decisive issues the reader must decide in assessing her book's thesis.

Critical Questions

1. Has Keen made a convincing case that we can sep-arate specific biblical rules from the principles they embody as discretely as she presumes?

2. Is Keen correct that a specific rule cannot itself be a universal principle but must always be the em-bodiment of a more abstract principle? That is to say, is it *impossible* that a specific rule could do

double duty as a universal principle? For example, consider these rules: "Never betray an innocent friend to death" or "You shall not commit adultery."

3. Does limiting inspiration to general principles while attributing all applications to culturally conditioned human judgments do justice to the Bible as a whole, especially from an evangelical perspective?

4. Has Keen made a sufficient case that these so-called universal principles are not merely abstractions that give no specific guidance in real-life situations but depend for their content on subjective or cultural factors? For example, does "Always love" mean "Never participate in any act that makes another person feel unhappy?" Even if we take it to mean, "Always seek the best for everyone," within what moral framework do we determine what is best?

5. If the only inspired moral guidance in the Bible is that articulated in the universal principles listed by Keen and those principles lie behind the law codes of every nation—ancient Babylon, Egypt, Greece, India, and China—what sense does it make to claim divine inspiration for their presence in the Bible? Will evangelicals be satisfied with such a theory of inspiration? It seems more like a theory of natural law written on every heart than the special revelation that evangelicals treasure.

6. Designer Interpretation II

In chapter 5 ("What is Ethical? Interpreting the Bible Like Jesus"), Keen puts the finishing touches on her theory of biblical interpretation.[21] She devotes the rest of the book to its application.

---

[21]In her more recent book on biblical interpretation, Keen says, "The hermeneutical key, then, is the humility of God and our imitation of it. God shares power and serves us. To know God is to do the same. *If the Bible reading does not result in using our agency to elevate and serve others, we aren't doing it right.* Any approach to interpretation can be used for selfish ambition; the right reading is the one that embodies humility [*The Word of a Humble God: The Origins, Inspiration, and Interpretation of Scripture* (Grand Rapids: Eerdmans, 2022), p. 173, emphasis added]. I do not object in principle to the hermeneutics of humble love. The Bible clearly teaches that disciples of Jesus should be both humble and loving. Scripture should not be used as an instrument of torture. However, I object to Keen's implication that any interpretation of Scripture that causes unhappiness and shame in someone is for that reason alone wrong. This principle is too broad to be of any practical help. In many cases, helping people to recognize and repent of their wrong and destructive behaviors–even if it causes them to be sad or angry–can be an act of profound humility and deep love. The question, then, turns not only on whether an interpretation causes someone to be unhappy but on whether the condemned behavior is wrong.

Virtue Matters

In addressing the question of how the Bible teaches morality, Keen mentions commands, examples, symbolic worlds, and virtues. Virtue seems to be Keen's all-encompassing category. "Virtues," she explains, "are about *who* a person is, whereas rules address *what* a person does" (p. 56). Biblical virtues are culturally transcendent whereas laws and rules are culturally relative. Loving God and your neighbor are always right. In commenting on Jesus's statement, "But now as for what is inside you—be generous to the poor, and everything will be clean for you" (Luke 11:41), Keen draws the following principle:

> Jesus indicates that if we act out of virtue, the outcome is always the will of God…When the virtue of selfless love fills a person's heart, all actions that flow from that are pure and are pleasing to God. (p. 57)

Applying the above principle to same-sex relationships, Keen argues,

> If sin is defined as something that violates the fruit of the Spirit, how are loving, monogamous same-sex relationships sinful? These partnerships are fully capable of exhibiting the fruit of the Spirit. If Jesus says that all the law can be summed up in love, then don't these relationships meet this requirement? (p. 57)

Interpretation within the Bible

Keen finds the argument from virtue "compelling," but realizes that some in her target audience may need more convincing. To provide that extra push she attempts to demonstrate that the biblical authors themselves employ the very interpretive strategy she has been advocating. She examines three instances of such internal rereading of the Bible: Deuteronomy 15:12-18 covers the same situation as does Exodus 21:2-11 but softens the law, making it more humane. The Gospel of Matthew (19:9) makes an exception to Jesus's strict teaching on divorce as recorded in Mark 10:11-12, and Paul adds another ground for divorce in 1 Corinthians 7:12-15. In reply to the Pharisees' accusation that Jesus and his disciples were breaking the Sabbath law by stripping grain from the heads of wheat and eating it, Jesus cites David's breaking the law by eating the holy bread of the sanctuary because of his hunger (Mark 2:23-28; Matthew 12:3-4). Jesus concludes, "The Sabbath was made for man, not man for the Sabbath" (Mark 2:27). Keen infers from Jesus's teaching about the Sabbath that "God's ordinances are always *on behalf of* people and not for the arbitrary appeasement of God's sensibilities" (p. 65). If the author of Deuteronomy, Jesus, and Paul were correct to read the Bible this way, surely we are permitted to do so. Hence, we are not only free but obligated to apply biblical laws "with attention to human need and suffering" (p. 66).[22]

Universal Principle?

In this chapter, Keen continues to build her case begun in the previous chapter for the clear distinction between the Bible's specific instructions, which are culturally relative, and the universal moral principles that those instructions attempt to embody. This time she appeals to the category of virtue. Virtues are habitual attitudes that guide moral behavior in specific circumstances. Biblical *virtues* are universal principles that apply everywhere and always. In contrast, the moral quality of *behaviors* depends on how well they embody the universal virtues in specific contexts. Keen offers Jesus's teaching about the purpose of the Sabbath and Matthew's and Paul's adaptation of Jesus's teaching on

---

[22]Brandan J. Robertson makes a similar argument, drawing on a hermeneutic of liberation from oppression. His interpretative principle allows him to dismiss biblical moral teachings that do not liberate and humanize sexual minorities. He concludes: "It is this combination of biblical ethical trajectories and experience that should lead contemporary Christians on the same theological journey of Peter and the earliest apostles. If the Spirit of God moves among LGBT+ people, who are Christians to stand in the way of the work of God? One can almost hear the Spirit speaking once again to the church today, saying, "Do not call unclean that which I have made clean," referring to Peter's vision of clean and unclean animals in Acts 10:15 [*The Gospel of Inclusion: A Christian Case for LGBT+ Inclusion in the Church,* rev. ed. Eugene, OR: Cascade, 2022, p. 55)].

divorce as biblical examples of the distinction between universal principles and their contextual application. Undoubtedly, Jesus and Paul did distinguish between principle and application and between virtue and act. No one I know denies this distinction. But Keen's case depends on transforming the admitted distinction into a dichotomy and incorporating it into an interpretive framework that allows *no exceptions.* For admitting the possibility of exceptions would weaken Keen's case for the biblical legitimacy of same-sex relationships; it would plunge her into endless debates about which specific biblical instructions are transcultural. She would need to develop interpretive criteria for deciding *this* question also. The process of interpretation would never end. But applying her no-exceptions interpretive method consistently would create even worse difficulties for her case. We could accept no biblical command at face value. The Christian ethicist would need to explain how each and every biblical rule can be justified on the basis of general principles. Objections, alternative interpretations, disputes, and accusations of rationalization or callousness are sure to multiply.

7. Write the Rules, Win the Game

In the first chapter of this book, I summarized the seven-part argument I see unfolded in Keen's book. The first three steps proposed a set of interpretive principles. In subsequent chapters, I traced in detail how she arrives at the principles that play an essential role in her argument for the biblical acceptability of loving, covenanted same-sex relationships. It should be clear by now that if you accept her hermeneutical rules, you must accept the theological conclusions generated by applying those rules. It won't surprise the reader that I am suspicious that the rules were designed to generate the desired conclusions. Hence, I will devote this chapter to critiquing Keen's hermeneutical principles.

Keen's Hermeneutical Rule Book

According to Keen's method of interpretation, promoting the principles of justice, kindness and love while minimizing human suffering is the divine purpose of the Bible's moral instructions. The well-being of individuals and the community is the point. When the Bible commands or prohibits specific moral behaviors, these instructions must be viewed as conditional applications of justice and love to specific circumstances. When circumstances change, therefore, the specific applications of those unchanging principles must also change. What the biblical authors thought was just, good, loving, kind and compassionate in *their* circumstances we may judge not to be so in *our* circumstances. Hence, we are obligated to exercise our reason to determine whether a biblical command applies to our setting in the same way it applied to its original situation. If applying a rule as written to our setting would cause suffering, injustice, indignity or any other form of harm, we must reformulate it in a way that avoids these negative consequences.

Five Critical Observations

First, Keen can assert that the Bible's condemnation of same-sex intercourse is subject to revision in view of our understanding of what is good and just because *every* biblical command is subject to our judgment. What other behaviors could be justified by these same principles? Why are murder, stealing, adultery, fornication, lying and all other forbidden behaviors wrong? Might they not be justified in circumstances where one believes that they do not cause harm or cause less harm than the available alternatives? Is there an end to such deliberation? Who decides?

Second, Keen is correct that the Bible recognizes the difference between general moral principles and specific cases of their application and that God gave his commands for our good. But Keen asserts something more: that *we can know* in what ways they are good for us and *how* they may be applied today to produce good outcomes. She leaves out of consideration the possibility that God's commands are good for us in ways that we cannot presently grasp. Are there not cases in which we should simply obey a command because we trust the one who gave it?

Third, the Bible does not support Keen's view of interpretation. Every reader of the Bible knows that there is great emphasis in the Bible on trust and obedience to divine commands even when we do not perceive their wisdom. The Bible praises unquestioning obedience as a virtuous quality; it never approves of questioning the wisdom and goodness of the law (Psalm 119). Were Adam and Eve justified in questioning God's command not to eat of the tree of the knowledge of good and evil? The command did not seem reasonable to them (Genesis 3:6). The angel of the Lord communicated God's approval of Abraham's faith and obedience to the divine command to sacrifice his son Isaac (Genesis 22:1-19). Or, listen to the words of Deuteronomy 4:

> Hear now, O Israel, the decrees and laws I am about
> to teach you. Follow them so that you may live...
> Observe them carefully, for this will show your
> wisdom and understanding to the nations....So be

careful to do what the Lord your God has commanded you; do not turn aside to the right or to the
left. Walk in all the way that the Lord your God has
commanded you. (Deuteronomy 4:1-32)

Does the Bible really support Keen's view that we have
the wisdom, perspective and right to judge every biblical rule by what we think is good and loving?

Fourth, general principles alone cannot guide us in
specific situations. How do the principles of justice,
peace, mercy and love, apart from specific commands
and a tradition of examples, doctrine and narratives,
give us concrete guidance in particular situations? What
is just? How do I love my neighbor? What are compassion and mercy? Consider again Keen's assertion,
which I quoted in a previous chapter: "When the virtue
of selfless love fills a person's heart, all actions that
flow from that are pure and are pleasing to God" (p.
57). Really? Can goodwill alone guide our actions so
that they are always "pure and pleasing to God"? I
don't think so. Consider Philippians 1:9-11, which says,

> And this is my prayer: that your love may abound
> more and more in knowledge and depth of
> insight, so that you may be able to discern what is
> best and may be pure and blameless for the day of
> Christ, filled with the fruit of righteousness that
> comes through Jesus Christ—to the glory and
> praise of God.

Notice that love must be informed about what is best.
Thus informed, it can produce lives that are "pure and
blameless." Good motives are not enough. For it is possible to do bad things for the best of motives and good

things for the worst of motives. Paul urges us, instead, to do the best things for the best motives. Desire to do good things must be enlightened by knowledge of what is truly good. From where does this wisdom come?

Fifth, I am not convinced that Keen has sufficiently differentiated her interpretive principle from the progressive principle of interpretation, something she has obligated herself to do by claiming to be an evangelical writing for evangelicals. Simply to say, as Keen does, that evangelicals hold these universal principles binding because God commanded them does not differentiate Keen's approach from progressive theology. Progressives might be more radical than Keen in their application of this hermeneutical principle but their principles are identical. In their radicalism, progressives can claim with some justification that they are being more consistent than Keen is with her starting point.

Conclusion

In these criticisms, I have not attempted to demonstrate that Keen's interpretive principle is altogether false. I readily admit that it contains elements of truth, which accounts for its power to persuade some people. Nor have I offered an alternative interpretive strategy to explain the Bible's moral teaching. As a minimum result, the five criticisms above show that Keen has not demonstrated that her method of interpretation will bear the weight she places on it. Specifically, she has not shown that the distinctions between universal and contextual, virtue and deed, purpose and application, and principle and embodiment apply to every specific biblical command in a way that justifies revising it in view of its supposed underlying divine purpose. Therefore, she has not yet demonstrated that her hermeneutic method applies to the biblical prohibition of same-sex intercourse. She will have to make this case independently. Does she succeed? I will address this question in my treatment of the final three chapters of her book.

8. The Burden of Proof

In this chapter I want to discuss an issue I raised in the Introduction: who bears the burden of proof, the advocate of LGBTQ+ affirmation or the traditionalist? In a court of law in a criminal case, the defendant is presumed innocent until proven guilty "beyond a reasonable doubt." The prosecutor bears the "burden of proof." There is no *logical* law, however, that says the one who affirms a proposition (for example, "The defendant committed the crime." Or, "God exists.") bears a greater burden of proof than one who denies that proposition. For to deny the proposition "God exists" is logically equivalent to affirming the proposition, "God does not exist." In the same way, there is no logical law that says defendants are more likely to be innocent than guilty. The reason prosecutors bear the burden of proof is that in our culture we believe that it is morally preferable to let a guilty person go free than to punish an innocent one. Hence by demanding that the prosecution bear the burden of proof we increase our certainty that justice will be served. Who bears the burden of proof in the discussion in which we are now engaged, the one who affirms the proposition, "Same-sex relationships are acceptable Christian ways of life" or the one who denies this proposition? Logically speaking, there is no distinction in the level of evidence required to affirm or to deny this proposition. Who bears the burden of proof? is not a logical question at all but a *rhetorical* one, dependent on the makeup of the audience the speaker wishes to persuade.

The Bible-Believing Audience

Keen's target audience of Bible-believing evangelicals approaches her book with the presumption that the Bible teaches that same-sex intercourse is immoral and that the ecumenical church has held this view for 2,000 years without dissent. Keen implicitly acknowledges this rhetorical situation by arguing as if she bears the burden of proof. For on the face of it, the Bible and tradition stand overwhelmingly against her contention. She has an uphill climb, and it seems that she is clear about that. Because Keen has willingly accepted the burden of proof and argues accordingly, I do not as a critic need to accept responsibility for defending the opposing proposition (that is, "same-sex relationships are *not* morally acceptable Christian ways of living") to fulfill my duty of dealing with Keen's argument responsibly. All I need to do is rebut her case. If you are an evangelical who holds the traditional view of same-sex relationships and Keen cannot move you to doubt that position, you have no logical, rhetorical or moral duty to explain why you remain unmoved.

The Progressive Audience

When the audience is comprised of progressives or simply a cross-section of popular American culture, the rhetorical situation is completely reversed. Within the past few years, beginning in about 2010, a consensus has formed in American and other Western cultures that places gay relationships on an equal footing with traditional married couples. In 2024, anyone who argues in a public forum for the traditional view of same-sex relationships bears an insurmountable burden of proof. The biblical teaching on same-sex relationships carries no weight at all. Arguments from natural law or physical complementarity or reproductive capacity are met with incredulity, if not derision. Progressive culture has decided that the self-attested experience of gay people is the highest authority possible for deciding the issue. Anyone who contests this self-authenticating experience or refuses to draw the correct conclusions from this testimony can do so only from irrational prejudice, hatred, or fear. Within our culture, expressing traditional views on same-sex relationships corresponds to speaking blasphemy in theocratic cultures, and it engenders the same sort of response. Under these conditions, argument is impossible, dissent is forbidden, and silence provokes suspicion.

A Nagging Question

Before I take up the last three chapters of her book, I need to ask a question to which I will return in my examination of those chapters. Keen and other LGBTQ+ affirming evangelicals present their arguments as founded on the same view of biblical authority as that held by their evangelical audience. Keen seems to accept the burden of proof in relating to that audience. But I wonder how much the plausibility of her argument depends on evangelicals having absorbed to some degree the progressive assumption that the self-authenticating experience of gay people is the final court of appeal when it comes to the moral acceptability of same-sex relationships. Would Keen's creative interpretations of biblical texts possess any plausibility with evangelicals were it not for the influence of progressive culture on them, that is, were they not already disposed to find her arguments plausible? The social pressure on evangelicals to conform to progressive orthodoxy is powerful, pervasive, and relentless. They face it in their schools and colleges, in the media, in the workplace, and in law. There is no escape, no respite. It takes extraordinary clarity and strength to accept social marginalization as the price of remaining faithful to the Christian vision of life. Keen offers a simple way out of this difficulty: you can keep your evangelical piety, your Trinitarian orthodoxy and your doctrine of Scripture while joining progressive/popular culture in celebrating same-sex relationships. No doubt, this solution will appeal to many evangelicals, especially to younger generations. Does Keen consciously or unconsciously appeal to this desire for a way out? The cultural wind is clearly at Keen's back. To what extent does she take advantage of it to move her audience toward her position? These questions have been eating at me from the beginning.

9. Celibacy is Difficult

In her chapter 6 ("The Question of Celibacy for Gay and Lesbian People"), Keen deals with the question of celibacy. The first sentence of the chapter states well the question that drives the argument: "Does the difficulty of life-long celibacy provide biblical grounds for considering same-sex relationships morally acceptable?" (p. 68). Keen answers yes. How does she arrive at this conclusion? Does she make a compelling case?

Exceptions

Keen reminds readers that the Bible and evangelical churches make exceptions to moral rules under certain circumstances. In normal circumstances divorce is forbidden, but Paul allows divorce in the case of abandonment (1 Corinthians 7:15). In this circumstance, the option of saving the marriage does not exist. Thoughtful evangelicals, who view abortion as a terrible evil, recognize that in a situation where saving the life of the mother will come at the cost of her unborn child, abortion is permissible. You cannot save both. Keen applies this principle, derived from these and other extreme cases, to less extreme situations. In 1 Corinthians 7:1-7, Paul instructs married couples not to use their devotion to God as an excuse to deprive one another of sexual fulfillment. Paul advises unmarried people to remain unmarried, but if they are unable without great distress to remain celibate, they are free to marry. According to Keen, Paul thereby makes a compassionate concession to human weakness by approving marriage as an alternative to unhappy celibacy.

Celibacy as "Suffering"

To prepare the reader for application of Paul's situational thinking to same-sex relationships, Keen points to the likenesses between gay and heterosexual relationships. According to Keen, long pastoral experience and recent psychological studies have demonstrated that being gay is not a choice and can very rarely be changed. Moreover, single gays who attempt to remain celibate, like single heterosexual people who make this attempt, usually fail. Hence traditional alternatives to forming covenanted same-sex relationships within which sexual fulfillment can be achieved are unrealistic. For most gay people, marriage to a person of the opposite sex is not a workable option, and changing one's orientation is nearly impossible. In Keen's estimation, then, celibacy is not feasible for most gay people; it produces a kind of "physical and emotional death" (p.

71). It works against our God-created natures: "But the reality is that human beings are biologically made for sexual relationships, not life-long celibacy" (p. 74). "God created us with a strong familial drive to couple with another person and build a home" (p. 80).

Paul's Compassion

Keen now closes the loop. Paul understands that most single people cannot without great unhappiness devote themselves to a life of celibacy. In view of temptation to fornication and compassion in view of the suffering involved in celibacy, he permits them to marry, even though he thinks that in the present circumstances it would be better to remain single (1 Corinthians 7:29-31). Keen argues that Paul's logic can be applied to gay people. Given the divinely created drive to "couple with another person" (p. 80) for companionship and sexual fulfillment, the pain of celibacy and the lack of alternatives, the Pauline concession to marry can be applied to gay people as a "humanitarian" exception to the rule. Keen is not arguing that if Paul were confronted with the predicament of contemporary gay people and armed with the new knowledge we possess about sexual orientation, he would come to her conclusion.[23] No one can know what Paul would do. She argues, rather, that if we exercise the same concern for human weakness

---

[23]Progressives don't care, and affirming evangelicals don't dare.

and compassion for suffering that Paul exercised in 1 Corinthians 7, we will come to the conclusion she does. We will provide a way out of the "ethical dilemma of the gay person unable to achieve celibacy" (p. 82).[24]

Traditionalists' Cruelty

For the most part, Keen admirably refrains from impugning the character of her traditionalist opponents. Near the end of this chapter, however, she slips into an accusatory mood. The contemporary church's lack of sympathy for the plight of its gay members, she speculates,

> …stems from traditionalists' bias towards concerns more familiar to the majority of church members… their neglect of gay and lesbian people and their plight reflects traditionalists' grievous disregard of minority church members' needs—not unlike the early church's favoritism of Hebrew widows over Hellenistic widows during food distribution (Acts 6:1-4). [p. 81]

In making this accusation, Keen draws a not-so-subtle analogy between traditionalists' rejection of same-sex relationships and such ugly prejudices as racism and sexism. Why does she insert these barbs? Is she

---

[24]Keen misuses the idea of a dilemma. A logical dilemma is a forced choice between two false alternatives and a moral dilemma is a forced choice between two morally wrong alternatives. Keen poses the dilemma as between two unpleasant choices, but neither is false or morally wrong.

"preaching to the choir" of people who already agree with her conclusions? Or, is she appealing to those evangelicals who have already been influenced by progressive culture's successful categorization of gay people as an oppressed minority? (The "nagging question" I mentioned above.) In any case, it seems out of character with the thrust of the book. Keen concludes the chapter with an answer to the question with which she opened: "By extrapolating from Paul's instruction that people with strong passions should marry, a case can be made for the moral acceptability of same-sex covenanted relationships" (p. 82).

Keen's Argument for Compassion Examined

In her chapter 6, Keen argues:

1. If Paul makes exceptions to moral rules to accommodate human weakness and to spare single people the suffering of celibacy, we may also make such exceptions under similar circumstances.

2. Paul makes such exceptions.

3. Hence we may also make such exceptions to moral rules in similar circumstances.

4. Contemporary Christian gay people find themselves in a predicament similar to the predicament

of those people for whom Paul made exceptions to otherwise binding moral rules.

5. Hence we may make an exception to the moral rule against same-sex relationships for Christian gay people for whom other alternatives are not possible or would cause grievous suffering.

Critical Observations

Keen's five-step argument begins with a hypothetical proposition in which the truth of the second clause depends on the truth of the first. But proposition #2 is false. Paul does not make *exceptions* to moral rules based on the circumstances described in 1 Corinthians 7. In the case of divorce, he simply acknowledges that abandonment by the unbelieving partner constitutes a de facto divorce unrelated to a decision made by the believer. With regard to Paul's advice for single people to marry if they cannot remain celibate, Paul never asserts that celibacy is a moral requirement for anyone. Hence permission to marry is not an *exception* to a moral rule. If Paul does not in either of these cases make an exception to a moral rule, he sets no precedent and gives no guidance about how to make exceptions to moral rules. The similarity stated in proposition #4 is only superficial. Hence the conclusion made in proposition #5 is unwarranted, and Keen's argument goes nowhere.

10. Gay Orientation

In her chapter 7 ("Is it Adam's Fault? Why the Origin of Same-Sex Attraction Matters), Keen argues that one's view about the origin of same-sex attraction matters in assessing its moral status. She rejects two options on the issue of origins and settles on a third.

Moral Fallenness

The first view asserts that same-sex attraction is rooted in our "moral fallenness," that is, the universal tendency to sin inherited from Adam. In this case, same-sex desire falls into the same category as other such sinful desires as lust, pride, greed, envy, and hate. Individuals are morally culpable both for the desire and the acts that gratify the desire. We are obligated not to act on these desires and to purify our hearts of them insofar as possible. Keen rejects the first option as untenable exegetically and theologically and erroneous according to the best scientific understanding of human origins. According to Keen, the story of the creation and fall of human beings in "Genesis portrays a theological and not a scientific account of human origins" (p. 87).

Natural Fallenness

The second option locates the origin of same-sex attraction in "natural fallenness." Natural fallenness refers to the divine "curse" resulting from the fall (Genesis 3) and includes sickness, death, and natural evils. On this reading, same-sex attraction falls into the same category as birth defects, chemical imbalances, abnormal brain development, genetic diseases, and other deviations from health of body and mind. Those afflicted with such ills had no choice in the matter. Keen seems to think the second option is an improvement over the first, because it does not attribute same-sex attraction to a morally corrupt nature or malicious choices. Drawing on her hermeneutical studies in previous chapters, Keen argues that evangelical believers ought to accommodate this "disability" in the same way they accommodate other "imperfections" that affect people. Allowing gay people to form "covenanted relationships" for "companionship and support" would be the most helpful way to enable people "to live with the actual bodies they have" (p. 96). It is clear, however, that Keen does not think this view accounts for all the biological, psychological and experiential data, for it implies that gay people are defective in some way. Nor does it embody justice, because Gay Christians would inevitably be treated as second class citizens of the kingdom of God.

Natural Variation

The third option, clearly preferred by Keen, treats same-sex attraction as a natural variation within the human population, morally neutral and non-disabling. Only about ten percent of the human population, for example, is left-handed. Historically, left-handed people were considered flawed and devious. Even in the modern era, parents and therapists attempted to "fix" left-handed people. Recently, however, the Western world has come to a consensus that "there is nothing wrong with being left-handed" (p. 97). Keen recommends that Christians view same-sex desire in the same way we view left-handedness, as a natural variation that consistently characterizes three to five percent of the population. It is not a sin or a curse but a "gift of difference" (p. 97).

Analytical Thought

Keen's argument progresses from a viewpoint that roots same-sex desire in Adam's sin to a view that roots it in the negative effects of Adam's fall to a view that denies altogether the immoral or defective nature of same-sex desire. As Keen represents it, the first view taints same-sex attraction with the sinful character of its origin in Adam's sin. The second view removes the taint of sin from same-sex attraction but leaves unchanged its status as a defect caused by the sin of Adam. The third view, however, roots same-sex desire in undefined, chance variations within natural processes. Keen draws the following conclusion, which I have summarized in my own words: *Since the origin of same-sex desire is morally neutral, the desire itself is morally neutral, and if the desire is morally neutral, acting on the desire is also morally neutral.*

Notice how the force of Keen's final conclusion depends on a connection made in the first option between the origin of same-sex attraction and its present moral status. As she represents them, traditionalists ground their knowledge of the sinful nature of same-sex attraction in their speculative view of its sinful origin in the fall. This is not true. To the contrary, traditionalists assume that the origin of same-sex attraction must be sinful *because they already believe* from biblical moral teaching that same-sex intercourse and the desires that lead to it are sinful. That is to say, the moral character of the origin of a desire is revealed by the manifest moral character of the act arising from the desire, not the other way around. Likewise, Keen can speculate in the third option that the origin of same-sex attraction is morally neutral *only because she already believes* that same-sex attraction is morally neutral on other grounds. She knows that same-sex attraction cannot be a divine curse following on the sin of Adam because she knows on other grounds that it is not a curse at all. What are these other sources of Keen's knowledge that same-sex attraction is morally neutral?

Conclusion

As articulated by Keen, all three options beg the question. They assume from the beginning what they ostensibly set out to prove, moving in one giant circle. Contrary to her intentions, Keen's chapter 7 teaches us that speculation about the origin of a characteristic cannot help us determine its present moral status. Theological reasoning moves in the reverse direction.

11. Imagine

In her chapter 8 ("Imagining a New Response to the Gay and Lesbian Community"), Keen makes her final appeal for changes in the way evangelical believers relate to gay Christians. She opens the chapter by summarizing her foregoing conclusions and urging readers to allow the following principles to inform the debate:

> Proper interpretation of Scripture requires recognizing the overarching intent of biblical mandates, namely, a good and just world. (p. 102)

> Scripture itself teaches us that biblical mandates, including creation ordinances, cannot be applied without a deliberative process. (p. 102)

> Evidence indicates that life-long celibacy is not achievable for every person. (p. 103)

> Evidence shows that same-sex attraction is not moral fallenness; it could be understood as natural fallenness or human variation. (p. 103)

Practical Options

On the basis of these four assertions, which are the conclusions to which the previous chapters have come, Keen argues that there are three ways evangelicals can embrace same-sex relationships without abandoning their evangelical faith: First, the "traditionalist exception" position enables even those who believe that same-sex relationships are wrong to accept them as accommodations to human weakness because covenanted, loving relationships are better than promiscuity. Second, the "traditionalist case-law" view accepts the principle that we must take into account the "overarching intent" of biblical mandates. Given that many gay people cannot remain celibate and that their determination to live good lives would be greatly strengthen by remaining within the Christian community, traditionalists could view such relationships as morally acceptable. Third, the "affirming" view accepts gay relationships on the same basis as those between other-sex couples. The affirming view considers the biblical prohibitions against same-sex relationships to be "prescientific" in the same way it sees the biblical cosmology as prescientific. The affirming view bases its acceptance of same-sex relationships not on the letter but on the intent of biblical sexual regulations. For the Bible's rules for sex are designed to prevent harm and facilitate "a good and just world" (p. 51). "But same-sex relationships are not harmful by virtue of their same-sex nature" (p.

106), Keen adds.[25] They become harmful in the same way other-sex relationships become harmful, that is, when they are poisoned by betrayal, violence, coercion, deception, manipulation, and other unloving acts.

Karen Keen's "Personal Journey"

In the last section of the book, Keen recounts the journey from her introduction as an infant to "a small-town conservative Baptist church" (p. 108) to the frightening—in some ways shattering—experience in her late teens of "falling in love" with her best female friend (p. 109). Keen continues her story by recounting some of the stages in her twenty-year quest to understand herself as gay and Christian. I will not attempt to summarize in detail Keen's story. I could not possibly do justice to the confusion and loneliness that at times show through her rather straightforward account. Her book is the fruit of her intellectual journey...so far.

---

[25]I find this claim astounding. It begs one of the most important questions of her argument. She seems to argue that since same-sex relationships as such do not cause harm, the Bible texts that seem to condemn them don't really do so. The traditionalist argues the opposite: since the Bible condemns them as such, they must be harmful.

Analytical Thoughts

Theoretical or Practical?

From the beginning, I've been struck by the way Keen combines arguments from biblical exegesis and interpretation and lived experience with her practical goals. In her last chapter we see highlighted Keen's practical, pastoral side. Clearly, she would prefer that evangelicals accept her case for affirming loving, covenanted, same-sex relationships on the same basis as other-sex loving, covenanted relationships. But she is willing to tolerate the "traditionalist exception" and "traditionalist case-law" views as ways to include same-sex couples in the life of the church without them having to deny their identities or struggle unhappily to remain celibate. Keen will not allow desire for ideological purity to stand in the way of achieving her practical aim. I am only speculating here, but perhaps she hopes that once churches allow gay relationships, even on a less than ideal basis, they may be persuaded to move on to the "affirming" view by coming to understand gay people on a personal level.

The Rhetoric of Autobiography

It is foolish as well as insensitive to argue with someone's telling of their story or to diminish the significance of their self-reported experiences. People feel what they feel. No one knows this better than they do. The quickest way to alienate a contemporary audience is to appear unsympathetic to anyone society has designated a victim of oppression. Hence it is almost impossible for members of recognized oppressed groups to resist using their stories of struggle and oppression to prove that they are on the right side of history; anyone not sympathetic with them is by that very fact on the wrong side. I appreciate very much that Karen Keen for the most part resists this temptation. Along with everyone else, she knows that feeling that something is good or right or true does not make it so. Things are good or true or right independently of our private experiences. To assume otherwise would destroy the very idea of morality. Nor can telling one's story serve as proof for anything other than the subjective experience of the storyteller. A listener has no rational or moral obligation to accept a story full of pathos as proof of anything other than the emotional state of the storyteller. Such stories rightly evoke compassion but cannot legitimately command agreement.

It would take a hard heart indeed not to be moved by Karen Keen's story. Her first church experience, not unlike my own, was of a small, very traditional, and Bible-centered congregation. She wanted to become a missionary, and I wanted to preach the gospel in the church. I too made a journey through graduate study of the Bible and theology, confronting all the critical questions modern historians, biblical scholars, philosophers, and theologians raise about the faith. I am also passionate about healthy teaching in the church and the care of the little lambs in Jesus's flock. We both published books with Eerdmans Publishing Company. I do not, however, have her experience of being a woman or of having same-sex attraction. I do not consider myself better than her on this account. I know that I am worthy only to pray the tax collector's prayer, "God be merciful to me, a sinner." This is also my prayer for everyone, including Karen Keen. Since I read her book the first time and looked at her website, I've felt a great love for her. I find her story compelling in many ways. Nevertheless, for all the reasons I've laid out in this book, I find myself unmoved by her argument that accepting same-sex relationships is consistent with a Bible-based evangelical faith.

Part Two: Progressive Theology: The Silent Partner

In Part One, I unfolded Karen Keen's argument for the compatibility of biblical faithfulness with affirmation of covenanted gay relationships. I documented how she summarizes traditionalist and progressive interpretations of the biblical texts that have been cited as proof that the Bible condemns same-sex sexual activity. Traditionalists argue that these texts show clearly that the Bible condemns all forms of same-sex intercourse. Progressives argue that the Bible has in view only abusive or idolatrous acts; it does not address loving, faithful, covenanted same-sex unions. Keen asserts that the debate between traditionalists and progressives ends in a "stalemate" (p. 43). She writes her book to move the debate beyond this impasse. As I pointed out, however, Keen spends three times more space on progressive interpretations than on traditionalist ones. Progressive exegesis plays a pivotal role in her argument as a way to neutralize traditionalist exegesis. For her argument goes nowhere if she allows traditional interpretations to stand. But as an evangelical, she cannot simply take the progressive side against the traditionalists. What to do? Not to put too fine a point on it, she employs progressives to do her dirty work, keeping her hands clean and her evangelical vestments unsoiled. Progressive mercenaries having fought her battle with traditionalists to a draw, Keen is now free to tip the "stalemated" scales toward accepting same-sex relationships without offending evangelical sensibilities.

In Part Two, comprised of three chapters, I will examine one example of the progressive biblical interpretation on which Keen depends. This examination will call into question her contention that she has mapped out a stable theological position between progressive and traditional theology. As it turns out, her position is quite wobbly, because you cannot accept the moral authority of self-reported experience as the interpretive key to the Bible's moral teaching without at the same time rejecting the evangelical view that the Bible is the definitive authority for Christian faith and practice. Finally, I will urge the church to reject calls, such as that by Keen, to affirm gay relationships on the same basis as traditional marriage.

12. Progressive Biblical Interpretation

In this chapter, we will examine a prominent progressive scholar's take on the texts most used by traditionalists to condemn same-sex relations. In doing so, we will get a peek behind the curtain at the work on which Keen depends to neutralize traditional exegesis. Robert K. Gnuse is a progressive Lutheran advocate of affirming same-sex relationships. In his article "Seven Gay Texts: Biblical Passages Used to Condemn Homosexuality," Gnuse aims to demonstrate that "there is no passage in the biblical text that truly condemns a sexual relationship between two adult, free people, who truly love each other" (p. 85).[26] Hence, the biblical passages that are traditionally used to condemn homosexual acts are irrelevant to the modern debate and "should not be called forth in the condemnation of gay and lesbian people in our society today" (p. 85). I will not take the space to do a full analysis of the very sophisticated historical and exegetical aspects of his argument. Other

[26]*Biblical Theology Bulletin* 45. 2 (May 2015): 68-87.

authors have already done a good job replying to progressive interpretation of these texts.[27] I will concentrate, rather, on the theological conclusions he draws from his exegetical work and its implications for a possible gay-affirming evangelicalism.

The Curse of Ham (Genesis 9:20-27)

In this passage, one of the three sons of Noah looked on the naked body of his drunk father. After Noah sobered up, he cursed Ham and his descendants. It is sometimes argued that Ham performed some sort of homosexual act on his unconscious father. The story is taken, then, to condemn homosexual acts in general. In response to this theological use of the text, Gnuse points out that even if the text speaks of a homosexual act, it is also an act of incest and rape. The passage, then, cannot be used to condemn same-sex activity in general.

---

[27]For extensive, scholarly refutation of progressive interpretation of the "gay texts," see the books I mentioned in the Introduction: Robert A. J. Gagnon, *The Bible and Homosexual Practice: Texts and Hermeneutics* and Rubel Shelly, *Male & Female God Made Them: A Biblical Review of LGBTQ+ Claims.*

Sodom (Genesis 19:1-11; compare Judges 19:15-28)

This passage tells the story of the visit of two angels (apparently disguised as men) to the house of Lot and the demand by the men of the city of Sodom that Lot give his visitors to them so that they can rape them. Lot offers the men of the city his daughters instead, but the men angrily insist on having the visitors. In response, the angels struck the men with blindness. This story has been presented as proof of the Bible's severe condemnation of homosexuality, so much so that the name of the city became a designation for homosexual acts and persons: Sodomy and Sodomite. Gnuse points out that homosexual rape (by heterosexuals) of strangers, slaves and foreigners was common in the ancient world as a way of humiliating and subjugating vulnerable people. According to Gnuse, then, this passage condemns the men of Sodom for attempting to rape Lot's visitors to whom he had given shelter. It "has nothing to do with homosexuality between free consenting adults in a loving relationship" (p. 73).

Leviticus 18:21-24 and 20:13

Leviticus 18: 21–24 condemns three practices: sacrificing children to Molech, same-sex intercourse, and bestiality. Verse 22 addresses same-sex intercourse: "You shall not lie with a male as with a woman; it is an abomination." Traditionally, verse 22 has been taken as a clear condemnation of homosexual intercourse in general. And, apart from consideration of the context, verse 22 seems to condemn all forms of this behavior, no matter what the circumstances. Gnuse, however, argues that this verse may be directed to practices common in the cultic worship of Canaanite gods. Interestingly, Gnuse admits the possibility that the prohibition could refer to homosexual relations in general. But even if it does so, Gnuse attributes the prohibition to the Israelite obsession with maximizing population growth "because as a people they always faced a chronic population shortage" (p. 76). Implicit in Gnuse's explanation is the thought that waste of sperm and absence of reproduction are the real sins, not the same-sex acts themselves. If these concerns were removed, as they are in contemporary circumstances, the text would lose its force as a general moral rule. I will make one critical observation at this point. Notice that verse 21 does not explicitly condemn child sacrifice in general, but only that made to Molech. According to the reasoning employed by Gnuse in dealing with verse 22, verse 21 leaves open the possibility of sacrificing children to gods other than Molech.

Leviticus 20:13 says, "If a man lies with a male as with a woman, both of them have committed an abomination; they shall be put to death, their blood is upon them." On the face of it, this text condemns in very harsh terms homosexual intercourse in general. Gnuse takes this text also to refer to cultic prostitution, which would involve worshiping a Canaanite god or goddess. Gnuse concludes: "The real question is what the text really condemns, whether it be all homosexual behavior or cultic homosexual behavior. If it is cultic homosexual behavior, we should not use it in the modern debate" (p. 78).

How to "Theologize" Based on Biblical Texts

Gnuse's replies to Robert Gagnon's argument *(The Bible and Homosexual Practice,* Abingdon Press, 2001) that the Old Testament moral perspective at work in the texts and in the background culture condemns all forms of homosexual behavior. Gnuse's reply is worth quoting in full:

> He is probably correct about the cultural assumptions of that age, and maybe even about the attitudes of the biblical authors. However, we theologize off of the texts, not the cultural assumptions of the age or something the biblical authors may have thought but did not write down....The homosexual texts, and the laws in particular, do not lead us anywhere; they simply prohibit certain forms of activity. But the bottom line is that we theologize off the texts, not our scholarly reconstruction of the cultural values of the authors. The texts appear to condemn rape and cultic prostitution, not generic homosexuality; we should not therefore conclude that all homosexual behavior is condemned. (p. 78)

In constructing Christian ethics, maintains Gnuse, we are limited to what the biblical writers actually say about the circumstances at hand, not what we think they would say about other circumstances. Because the Bible does not explicitly condemn loving, adult same-sex relationships, we ought not to condemn them either, even though we can surmise that the biblical authors would have condemned them had they been asked about them.

I doubt that Gnuse (or Keen) can consistently apply this very legalistic rule to his own interpretation. The rule seems designed to make these "gay" texts irrelevant to the current debate. Moreover, it seems to me that this principle of theological interpretation makes it nearly impossible to argue successfully that the Bible teaches any ethics at all. For the Bible never speaks directly to contemporary circumstances. On any moral topic, we can always assert that circumstances today differ from those addressed in these ancient texts.

Vice Lists (1 Corinthians 6:9-10 & 1 Timothy 1:8-11)

The vice list passages read as follows:

> Do you not know that wrongdoers will not inherit the kingdom of God? Do not be deceived! Fornicators, idolaters, adulterers, male prostitutes, sodomites, thieves, the greedy, drunkards, revilers, robbers—none of these will inherit the kingdom of God. (1 Corinthians 6:9-10; NRSV)

> Now we know that the law is good if one uses it legitimately. This means understanding that the law

> is laid down not for the innocent but for the lawless
> and disobedient, for the godless and sinful, for the
> unholy and profane, for those who kill their father
> or mother, for murderers,
> fornicators, *sodomites,* slave traders, liars, perjurers,
> and whatever else is contrary to the sound teaching
> that conforms to the glorious gospel of the blessed
> God, which he entrusted to me. (1 Timothy 1:8-11;
> NRSV)

The Greek words that are translated "male prosti-tutes" *(malakoi)* and "sodomites" *(arsenokoitai)* in 1 Corinthians 6:9 may refer to the passive and the active partners in same-sex male intercourse. According to Gnuse, the NRSV translation of *"malakoi"* implies that these men allow sex to be performed on them for mon-ey. Or perhaps they are slaves who have no choice. The translation of *arsenokoitai* as "sodomites" implies that these men are abusers of some type, and may imply men who have sex with young boys. Gnuse concludes that when the two words are grouped together

> …we have the two words that describe the homo-sexual relationships that would have been observed
> most frequently by Paul. These were the master, old
> man, abusive sexual partner, or pederast on the one
> hand, and the slave, young boy, or victim on the
> other hand…Ultimately, I believe both words de-scribe abusive sexual relationships, not loving rela-tionships between two adult, free males. (p. 80)

Gnuse interprets 1 Timothy 1:10 in much the same way as he interpreted 1 Corinthians 6:9. The word *ar-*

senokoitais is also used in this passage. Gnuse again concludes that

> Homosexual love between two adult, free males or females may not be described here…[the New Testament] is condemning the violent use of sex to degrade and humiliate people, not sexual inclinations. (p. 81)

Romans 1:22-28

Romans 1:22-28 is often taken as the most unequivocal condemnation of same-sex intercourse in general, male and female. Gnuse denies this conclusion. I will summarize the main thrust of his extensive argument. The text reads as follows:

> Claiming to be wise, they became fools; and they exchanged the glory of the immortal God for images resembling a mortal human being or birds or four-footed animals or reptiles. Therefore God gave them up in the lusts of their hearts to impurity, to the degrading of their bodies among themselves, because they exchanged the truth about God for a lie and worshiped and served the creature rather than the Creator, who is blessed forever! Amen. For this reason God gave them up to degrading passions. Their women exchanged natural intercourse for unnatural, and in the same way also the men, giving up natural intercourse with women, were consumed with passion for one another. Men committed shameless acts with men and received in their own persons the due penalty for their

error. And since they did not see fit to acknowledge God, God gave them up to a debased mind and to things that should not be done. (NRSV)

As with all the other passages he examines, Gnuse argues that Paul in Romans 1:22-28 does not speak "about all homosexuals; he is speaking about a specific group of homosexuals who engage in a particular form of idolatrous worship" (p. 81). Gnuse argues that Paul targets the immoral behavior characteristic of certain religious cults resident in Rome. Gnuse speculates that the most likely target for Paul's invective is the Egyptian Isis cult. Paul condemns idolatry as false, dark and foolish and asserts that this darkness gives birth to gross immorality unbefitting of one made in the image of God. If he condemns same-sex intercourse only because of its connection with idolatry, why does Paul call this idolatrous homosexual behavior "unnatural"? Traditional interpreters contend that Paul's argument makes no sense unless he assumes that homosexual behavior is immoral even apart from its connection to idolatry. Paul's point is that this cascade of immoral behaviors is what happens when people abandon the true God. These behaviors must be immoral in themselves. Otherwise, his critique of idolatry would fall flat. Paul wants his readers to understand that deserting God to worship creatures will lead to abandoning the created order of things. Bad things are sure to follow such abandonment.

In opposition to the traditional reading that uncouples homosexual behavior from idolatry, Gnuse insists that Paul critiques only those homosexual acts performed in worship to pagan gods. Why, then, does Paul label these acts "unnatural"? Gnuse answers: "What Paul would find offensive about this cultic behavior, besides the obvious worship of other gods, is that the sexual behavior did not bring about procreation; that is what makes it 'unnatural'" (p. 83). Gnuse has made a telling admission here. He admits that Paul *can* disengage homosexual acts from idolatry and view them negatively apart from their connection to pagan worship. They are "unnatural" everywhere and always and for everyone. But Gnuse's contention that Paul viewed them as "unnatural" only because they do not produce children makes it easy for him to dismiss Paul's judgment as cultural bias in favor of procreation as the sole purpose of sexual intercourse. It seems to me much more likely that Paul sees same-sex intercourse as "unnatural" because it violates the natural order intended by the creator and witnessed to by the power of procreation rooted in the obvious physical complementarity of the sexes. The foolish "exchange" of the glory of God for images of beasts (vss. 22-23) is mirrored by the degrading "exchange" of "natural intercourse for the unnatural" (v. 26).

What are the women mentioned in verse 26 doing when they "exchange natural intercourse for unnatural"? Gnuse points out correctly that Paul does not explicitly say that these women were having sex with other women, only that they were doing something "unnatural." Gnuse floats the possibility that Paul has in mind a form of heterosexual intercourse designed to prevent procreation. I think this hypothesis is unlikely given what Paul says about men in the next verse. In any case, Paul asserts that whatever these women are doing is "unnatural" and therefore wrong and shameful everywhere and always and for everyone.

Gnuse's Conclusion

Given what he said about each text individually, Gnuse's overall conclusion will not come as a surprise:

> I believe that there is no passage in the biblical text that *truly* condemns a sexual relationship between two adult, free people, who truly love each other.... [Hence] biblical texts should not be called forth in the condemnation of gay and lesbian people in our society. (p. 83; emphasis mine)

Comments

Notice the negative form of Gnuse's conclusion. He offers many alternative interpretations of these texts, some of which I mentioned. Many of them are tenuous and speculative. Some give the impression of plausibility, but as his conclusion indicates, the purpose of the article is not to defend any of these alternative interpretations. The entire discussion serves one purpose: *to raise doubts about* the traditional view that these passages unambiguously condemn same-sex intercourse. The goal is to make illegitimate any theological use of these texts in the modern debate over homosexuality. It is to "problematize" the interpretation of these texts, to draw traditionalists into interminable debates, which, because we cannot arrive at a conclusion that ends all debate, leave the impression that everyone is free to think whatever they wish and do whatever they want. If you continue to interpret these texts in the traditional way, you can plausibly be accused of homophobia, that is, of irrational animus toward gay people. Like Keen, Gnuse attempts to turn the tables on traditionalists by shifting the burden of proof onto those who would use "the gay texts" in Christian ethics to condemn all forms of same-sex intercourse. Gnuse writes as if all he needs to do to win the argument is show that the texts do not *explicitly* address adult, free, and loving same-sex relationships. They may be directed exclusively to same-sex behavior that is abusive, violent or idolatrous, or linked with some other behavior that modern people also find easy to condemn. If Gnuse can undermine the use of these biblical texts to condemn same-sex relations in general, traditionalists must abandon their strongest arguments and argue with progressives on their own turf where they are at a disadvantage, that is, from experience, science, psychology, and subjective feelings.

As I pointed out many times in this study, Keen and other gay-affirming evangelicals rely on the biblical exegesis of such progressive biblical interpreters as Robert K. Gnuse to neutralize traditionalists' appeal to the biblical teaching in the "gay texts." Keen and others deny that one must accept progressive theology in order to use progressive biblical interpretation. As we can see, however, both Gnuse and Keen bring to the texts the presupposition that we must not interpret them in a way that condemns relationships and behavior *we experience* as loving and healthy. This elevation of personal, subjective experience to a source of theological truth on par with Scripture is the very founding principle of progressive theology. The idea of a gay-affirming evangelicalism, if not a complete oxymoron, is a juxtaposition of two incompatible ideas. Modifying evangelicalism enough to make it compatible with "gay-affirming" theology will transform it into progressivism.

13. Progressive Logic

Not all progressive Christians are alike. Some reject or extensively revise the doctrines held dear by the historic tradition: the bodily resurrection of Jesus, the Trinity, the incarnation, and the call to conversion. I find it difficult to think of them as Christian at all.[28] Some are less radical in their revisions. What they all have in common, however, is that they feel compelled to revise traditional/biblical Christian doctrine and morals in view of modern culture. The dominant contemporary culture has given up all ethical principles by which it might condemn behaviors that do not involve coercion. The Enlightenment's emphasis on individual freedom, the Romantic Movement's emphasis on the uniqueness of the individual's inner self, and post-modernism's debunking of objective truth have come together in contemporary culture to create a picture of each individual as a self-creating god who can do anything it wants as long as it does not do violence to other self-creating

---

[28]See Roger Olson, *Against Liberal Theology: Putting the Brakes on Progressive Christianity* (Grand Rapids: Zondervan, 2022), for a treatment of the radical side of progressive theology, which in the past was called Liberal Theology.

gods. Progressive Christians try to adjust their theology and ethics to this culture. They are as embarrassed by traditional Christian moral teaching as they would be if they suddenly found themselves naked at a Kennedy Center opera performance.

At times, I wonder why progressive Christians even bother to appear to care what the Bible says. Traditionalists care what the Bible says because they place themselves under its authority and sincerely believe that God's speaks through the Bible. They want to participate in a community that lives according to the Bible's teaching. When progressives engage in sophisticated exegesis and hermeneutics, such as that we find in Gnuse's article, do they do this because they really care what the Bible says? Or, do they know already from the spirit of the times what the Bible should have said? I think some progressives work as hard as they do to reinterpret the Bible, not because *they* care what it teaches, but because *other* less enlightened people care and stand in the way of moral progress. Progressive efforts seem designed to undermine the certainty of traditional moral teaching while giving the appearance of sincere desire to understand the scriptures. In other words, progressive writing on biblical exegesis, hermeneutics and theological ethics strikes the traditionalist as dissimulation and deception. It will seduce only those who want to be seduced.

As we saw above, Robert K. Gnuse argues that the biblical proof texts most often quoted by traditionalists to condemn same-sex intercourse do not explicitly condemn *all* same-sex sexual relationships. These texts, progressives speculate, are most likely directed to abusive relationships common in the culture of that day. Because these passages do not mention loving gay relationships by name, progressives consider these scriptures irrelevant to the contemporary question about the Christian legitimacy of same-sex relationships. We do not know what Paul would say about loving gay relationships, progressives claim; we know only what he said about abusive same-sex relationships. Gnuse is not alone in adopting this line of argument. It is common among progressive Christian writers.[29]

It seems to me quite hypocritical for a progressive to argue in such a legalistic way. Progressives are not known for being sticklers for the letter of the law. Should we really believe that if the New Testament undeniably condemned all forms of same-sex intercourse, progressives would dutifully obey its teaching? I do not think so. Progressives also have many strategies for rejecting any New Testament teaching that conflicts with progressive culture. When clear New Testament teaching conflicts with progressive dogma, progressive writers complain that the New Testament authors were limited by their patriarchal, unscientific, homophobic, and

---

[29]Brandon J. Robertson, for example, says, "Even though I think our modern heterosexist reading of these texts is wrong and leads us to unfaithful conclusions, I have no problem conceding the fact that I believe Paul, a first century Jewish teacher, would likely have been condemning of same-sex relationships if he were to appear in our modern era with his first century worldview" [*The Gospel of Inclusion: A Christian Case for LGBTQ+ Inclusion in the Church*, rev. ed (Eugene, OR: Cascade, 2022), pp. 29-30].

sexist culture. When progressives pretend to care what Scripture teaches, they are throwing exegetical dust into the air and blowing hermeneutical smoke in traditionalists' eyes to hide the hypocrisy of their argument. For they have no intention of practicing what they preach.

Evangelical *and* Progressive?

Is it possible, as Keen and other LGBTQ+ affirming evangelicals contend, to use progressive exegesis and methods of interpretation in defense of their position without succumbing to the gravitational pull of progressive theology? I do not believe so, for several reasons. First, the plausibility of the evangelical affirming position depends on progressive exegesis, as we can see in Keen's use of it to neutralize traditional exegesis. If progressive exegesis depends on progressive theology, it follows that Keen's affirming stance also depends on progressive theology. It seems clear to me that the plausibility of progressive exegesis depends completely on the progressive view of religious authority. Progressives never tire of appealing to the so-called Wesleyan Quadrilateral.[30] According to this Anglican/Methodist tradition, there are four sources of theology: Scripture, tradition, reason, and experience. Each source plays an important part in the formation of doctrine. In its original form, the Quadrilateral acknowledged the primacy

---

[30]For more on the Quadrilateral, see Ted A. Campbell, W. Stephan Gunter, et. al., *Wesley and the Quadrilateral: Renewing the Conversation* (Nashville: Abington, 1997).

of Scripture and gave tradition an important but secondary place. Reason functions instrumentally, and experience confirms the truth of doctrine. In the progressive appropriation of the Quadrilateral, however, reason and experience are given authority equal to Scripture and tradition as "sources" of theology. Neither the progressive nor the evangelical drive to discover the affirming position in Scripture makes sense apart from experience-dependent claims about the unchangeability of same-sex orientation and the goodness of same-sex relationships. Progressives claim to learn from reason and experience that same-sex relationships are morally acceptable, so if the scriptures condemn these relationships, *the scriptures are mistaken.* Keen and other affirming evangelicals also claim that experience teaches that same-sex relationships are morally acceptable and assure us that the scriptures do not really condemn loving, covenanted same-sex relationships. Both groups, then, depend on giving reason and experience priority over Scripture and tradition. This reversal of priority opens the floodgates to many hitherto unimaginable possibilities, which leads to my third reason for doubting that the evangelical affirming position can resist the pull of full-blown progressive theology.

The careers of many "evangelical" affirming writers demonstrate a continual move toward progressivism. Brandon Robertson, for example, criticizes those evangelical advocates of inclusion who try to graft LGBTQ+ affirmation into an otherwise "conservative sexual ethics."[31] "Frankly," he quips, "I don't believe it is a sustainable or logical path...[for example] there is not a single verse that says sex is only intended for a marriage relationship" (p. 93). Applying the criterion of non-coercion and mutual love, Robertson concludes:

> At the heart of a Christian relational ethic should be the value of commitment and covenant, and many non-monogamous relationships are centered on a deep and enduring commitment of more than three people to walk in relationship with each other throughout life. Logically and ethically, I can see no reason to deem such relationships to be unethical or sinful. (p. 95)

Robertson distinguishes between polyamory and polygamy. Polyamory involves loving many sexual partners and is based on equality. Polygamy means having many wives in a patriarchal relationship. The former can embody the Christian vision of morality; the latter cannot. Robertson excludes prostitution, pedophilia, and bestiality from his list of Christian behaviors.[32] Evaluated by Robertson's criteria, Karen Keen seems like a naïve goody-two shoes who has not yet realized where her theological journey leads.

---

[31] *The Gospel of Inclusion*, p. 92.

[32] Robertson cannot escape the charge of incoherence he levels against others. By prioritizing experience over Scripture, he cannot sustain his rejection of the behaviors he lists and many others. I think especially of prostitution. What persuasive objection could he have against a person who wishes to make a living selling sexual satisfaction?

The career of David P. Gushee provides another striking example of the lure progressive logic has for evangelicals who cross the Rubicon of LGBTQ+ affirmation. In his 2014 book *Changing our Minds,* Gushee could still be described as an evangelical leader. The titles of his 2017 book *Still Christian: Following Jesus Out of American Evangelicalism* and his 2022 book *After Evangelicalism: The Path to a New Christianity* tell a story of change in the direction of progressive theology toward a perspective Gushee calls "post-evangelicalism."[33] In *After Evangelicalism,* Gushee proposes a two-tiered sexual ethic. Covenant marriage should be the aspirational norm by which every other use of sex is measured. In covenant marriage, people pledge to take care of each other through thick and thin. For all the reasons cultures down through the ages have encouraged it, marriage is still the best place to direct sexual energy toward personal and social wellbeing. Although Gushee does not mention gay marriage in this immediate context, it is clear that he includes these marriages within his category of covenant marriage. He says,

> I personally affirm that full acceptance of LGBTQ people is a nonnegotiable dimension of post-evangelical Christianity, and most others in this terrain seem to feel the same way. (p. 130)

Covenant marriage may be the ideal, says Gushee, but any workable sexual ethic must articulate a minimum as well as an ideal norm. Young unmarried people *will* have

---

[33]*After Evangelicalism,* p. 7.

sex, so we must provide guidance for those not ready for marriage. Gushee offers as a minimum standard this rule: sexual encounters should be conducted with "mutual enthusiastic consent," because "irresponsible, exploitative, and sadistic sexuality is extremely dangerous. It can deeply harm others and self" (p. 130). Marriage is Gushee's ideal, but he is willing to make "a concession to reality" (p. 134). If "legal marriage is unreachable or unwise," advises Gushee, it would nevertheless be "best" for partners "to structure long-term romantic-sexual relationships in a covenantal fashion" (p. 133).

At the end of his discussion of post-evangelical sexual ethics, Gushee finds himself resisting such LGBTQ+ advocates as Brandon Robertson and Nadia Bolz-Webber. He worries that Bolz-Webber engages in "overreaction to puritan perfectionism" in her liberated sexual ethic of non-coercive "sexual flourishing" (p. 134). According to Bolz-Weber, if you've been told that

> ...sexuality is good only if it is confined to a tiny circle, then you have been lied to, and I am sorry. God gave you your gifts and never intended for them to be buried. Whatever sexual flourishing looks like for you, that's what I would love to see happen in your life.[34]

Having abandoned the clarity of the traditional view of biblical authority, Gushee's objections to Robertson's approval of polyamory sound rather pathetic:

---

[34]Nadia Bolz-Weber, *Shameless: A Case for Not Feeling Bad About Feeling Good (About Sex),* reprint ed., (Convergent Books, 2020), p. 60.

With weary wisdom of my advanced years, I would counter that embracing polyamory on this basis [a polyamorous orientation] will weaken the case for LGBTQ+ equality. I would also suggest that polyamory is not likely to be a realistic option for sustainable, long-term covenant relationships. If children are involved or even possible, polyamory risks destabilizing their always-vulnerable lives. (p. 135)

What a long distance Gushee has traveled from the divine voice ringing out from Mount Sinai and Jesus's teaching in the Sermon on the Mount: "Thou shalt not commit adultery" (Exodus 20:14; Matthew 5: 27-28)!

14. The Choice

It is time to return to the question voiced in the subtitle of this book: *Should the Church Affirm LGBTQ+ Identities and Ways of Living?* It will not surprise anyone who has read the preceding chapters of this book that my answer is an unequivocal "No." As we have seen in our study of LGBTQ+ affirming writers, the church cannot do this without replacing the scriptures as the norm by which it measures its teaching with the subjective feelings, ideologies, and pseudo-sciences of progressive culture. Respect for the definitive authority of Scripture is the commonality that enables Christians among all nations, eras and traditions to reason together about how to think and live as Christians. Those who reject this principle separate themselves from this ecumenical discussion to become a heretical sect...even if they continue to speak reverently about Jesus, the kingdom of God, and the leading of the Spirit. By their fruits, not their words, you will know them!

The Question of Teaching Authority

How will the church decide this issue? Who will speak for the whole church? Individual believers, exegetes, and theologians? Local congregations and denominations? Individuals, of course, are free to construct their personal theological and ethical systems. But the opinions of individuals possess no authority for others. No Christian is obligated to accept an individual's opinion as binding Christian doctrine. The discussion about same-sex unions is ultimately about what doctrine the ecumenical church should teach and what moral behaviors it should require. In contemporary society a person is legally free to have sex with whomever they please as long as there is mutual consent. In this book I am not discussing sexual ethics for contemporary society. I am discussing whether or not the *church,* in obedience to Christ and following the leading of the Spirit, should affirm those who claim to be Christians and wish to participate in the life of the church while also living in a same-sex sexual relationship.

Christian denominations often acknowledge areas where diverse private opinions on theology are allowed and different areas where private choices of ways of life are permitted. But nearly all Christian denominations hold adherence to some doctrines necessary. Anyone who teaches a different doctrine is deemed a heretic. The recalcitrant person may be stripped of their office and excluded from teaching within the church. Likewise, anyone guilty of behaviors deemed by the denomination as immoral is subject to discipline. A person who rejects the church's moral teaching and teaches others to do the same may be subject to excommunication.

The Weight of Tradition

The church's doctrinal and moral teaching are the result of long-term communal reflection on Scripture, perhaps reaching all the way back to the apostles. Whereas most denominations do not hold their confessions of faith to be infallible, they are, nevertheless, slow to accept proposals for radical change. There is much to consider, too much for any one individual to grasp and too important to rush the process. On the matter of the moral status of same-sex unions, it would be difficult to find a moral or doctrinal teaching on which there is greater and longer-term consensus within the world-wide church. The church is right to be skeptical of proposals that interpret the scriptures in ways radically different from the way it has understood them for 2,000 years. As I demonstrated in my study of works by Karen Keen and Robert Gnuse, critics of the tradition can achieve no more than opening a mere possibility that the Bible does not condemn loving, non-coercive same-sex relationships along with its clear condemnation of exploitive same-sex intercourse. Gnuse admits that Paul probably would have condemned even non-coercive same-sex relationships, if he had been asked about them. The leap from these meager and speculative exegetical results to affirmation of same-sex unions as morally equal to traditional marriage is huge and completely unwarranted. It seems to me that those who make this giant leap do so for reasons other than desire to obey Scripture and use their exegetical gymnastics as a diversion to distract readers from the real reasons for their decision.

Church Decision Making

How does the church make decisions on doctrine and morals? The first thing on which to get clear is that the Christian church (Roman Catholic, Orthodox, or Protestant) has never claimed the freedom to create doctrine and moral law arbitrarily or to change it to fit the spirit of the age. Faithful churches acknowledge that they are charged with passing on the faith as they received it from Christ and his apostles. For my part, I will not acknowledge any institution as the church of Christ that will not make this confession or that I sense does not make it sincerely. Hence the church's decision-making process should focus on remaining faithful to the original gospel and moral vision in our present circumstances. I am suspicious of any church that seems to allow other concerns to divert it from this task. Churches, too, can be carried away by grave error and even become heretical.

The second thing to keep in mind is that the decision-making process of the church cannot be made completely formal. For example, it cannot be carried out through the mechanisms of direct democracy wherein a majority of the living members can legislate for the whole body. Nor is the church a representative democracy. It is certainly not a dictatorship. The goal is not to canvass the will of the people but to discern the will of God and seek God's guidance on how best to remain faithful in the present age. On matters that the church confesses and teaches, the community as a whole must come to consensus on the issue. This may take a long time. The process of coming to consensus may take place quite informally. Of course, on most doctrinal and moral issues, the present consensus was achieved centuries ago and has been reaffirmed by many succeeding generations of believers.

With respect to the challenge of those who argue that the church should affirm same-sex unions on the same basis as it affirms traditional marriage, what factors should the church consider? If it is determined to remain faithful, the church must continue to read Scripture as the standard of its faith and morals. Because it is open to deepening its understanding of God's will, the church will not refuse to listen to voices that propose new interpretations of Scripture. But the church did not begin to read Scripture yesterday. Hence it listens to those new interpretations only in light of what it has been taught by tradition. Tradition embodies the long-term, time-tested wisdom of the faithful about the meaning of the scriptures. A church that desires to be faithful will not discard it lightly. The burden of proof will always fall on those who challenge the wisdom of tradition. Moreover, the church will exercise discernment about whether or not these new voices speak with

sincere desire to seek the will of God or speak decep-
tively. Both Jesus and the beloved disciple tell us not to
be naïve about new teachings:

> Watch out for false prophets. They come to you in
> sheep's clothing, but inwardly they are ferocious
> wolves. By their fruits you will recognize them.
> (Matthew 7:15-16)

> Dear friends, do not believe every spirit,
> but test the spirits to see whether they are from
> God, because many false prophets have gone out
> into the world. (1 John 4:1)

Why Progressive Christianity Will Fail

Some readers may have come to agree with me that
Karen Keen and others have failed to show that one can
continue to adhere to the evangelical view of biblical
authority after having adopted the affirming position on
same-sex sexual relationships. But instead of renouncing the affirming stance, they may feel obligated to re-
nounce the evangelical view of biblical authority and
move into progressive Christianity. It may seem as if
this move will resolve the tension between evangelicalism and the compelling narratives of LGBTQ+ people.
I would like to warn against this move. The relief will
be temporary.

Progressive and post-evangelical writers propose a
"New Christianity," revised to conform to progressive
culture. Progressive Christianity recommends a new

sexual code, LGBTQ+ affirmation, a new understanding of the authority of Scripture, a social-justice Jesus, a non-omnipotent God, and an inclusive church. Progressives seem to think that the time is right for their message: young people are leaving evangelical churches in droves, tired of their moralistic, judgmental, dogmatic, and politically conservative agenda. Progressives offer their new Christianity to these "exiles" as an alternative to evangelicalism on the one hand and secularism on the other.[35] Progressives correctly observe that young people are dropping out of churches. Some of these dropouts give the reasons cited above. I am convinced, however, that the "New Christianity" being proposed by progressives is not Christianity at all; it is a counterfeit. I worry that many believers will be fooled by its likeness to the real thing. I've been told that recognizing a counterfeit one-hundred-dollar bill does not require knowledge of every possible mistake counterfeiters can make. It requires only detailed knowledge of authentic currency.

Sadly, few of these discouraged evangelicals possess thorough knowledge of original Christianity. They do not know the details or the central themes of the Bible, not to mention the story of church history...or history in general! Hence, they are vulnerable to clever reinterpretations of Bible texts and themes that do not fit the progressive narrative. Many will be deceived. In the

---

[35]For an example of such an invitation, see David A. Kaden, *Christianity in Blue: How the Bible, History, Philosophy, and Theology Shape Progressive Christianity* (Minneapolis: Fortress Press, 2021).

short term, I am pessimistic that I or other writers can stem the tide of the progressive movement. I feel like a person watching a slow-motion train wreck from a distance. No matter how much I yell no one listens and nothing changes. *In the long term, however, I am certain that progressive and post-evangelical Christianity will fail.* The main reason for my optimism is this: the continued existence of the Bible. Progressives cannot discard the Bible completely without renouncing their claims to be Christian. However, as long as the Bible can be found in bookstores, church pew racks, in libraries and in private residences, progressive Christianity faces the danger that some people will actually read it. When ordinary people read the Bible, they see that progressive Christianity is not the original, authentic Christianity but a fake. This thought gives me hope.

A Final Word

I cannot speak for the whole church or any particular congregation or denomination, and I possess no authority to obligate anyone to obedience. However, I urge believers individually and the church corporately not to be deceived by sophisticated arguments that, contrary to the unanimous Christian tradition and against the grain of reason, claim that Scripture does not condemn and perhaps even approves of same-sex unions. I believe these arguments possess moving force only for those already persuaded by the spirit of the age, which elevates the authority of a subjective sense of identity and

well-being above reason, moral law, traditional wisdom, and scriptural teaching. There are many obscure
areas of theology on which we can agree to disagree.
This is not one of them. As for me, I will not partner
with LGBTQ+ affirming churches or individuals. And I
urge all the faithful to consider doing likewise.

Afterword: On Ministering to Gay People

In the Introduction to this book, I let readers know in advance that I did not write to give practical advice to the church on its pastoral and evangelistic ministry to gay people. I do not possess the needed pastoral experience to do this. I limited myself to securing a good understanding of the doctrinal foundations for such ministries. However, lest readers mistake my doctrinal concentration for pastoral indifference, I feel compelled to say something about the practical implications of this book. Laying foundations makes no sense unless we build a structure on them. Hence, I want to urge the church to engage in ministry to LGBTQ+ people, and do so consistently with the doctrinal foundations I laid in this book.

The church's pastoral and evangelistic ministries should be conducted in love, truth, and wisdom. We must love gay people the way Jesus loved people. I've always been struck with Jesus's interaction with the rich man in Mark 10:17-22:

As Jesus started on his way, a man ran up to him and fell on his knees before him. "Good teacher," he asked, "what must I do to inherit eternal life?

"Why do you call me good?" Jesus answered. "No one is good—except God alone. You know the commandments: 'You shall not murder, you shall not commit adultery, you shall not steal, you shall not give false testimony, you shall not defraud, honor your father and mother.'"

"Teacher," he declared, "all these I have kept since I was a boy."

Jesus looked at him and loved him. "One thing you lack," he said. "Go, sell everything you have and give to the poor, and you will have treasure in heaven. Then come, follow me."

At this the man's face fell. He went away sad, because he had great wealth.

Jesus looked at him! He looked into his heart. And looking at him, Jesus *loved* him. I suppose he loved him for his zeal for God's law. But Jesus's love also involved compassion for the rich man's bondage to his wealth, which was holding him back from loving God with his whole heart, mind, soul, and strength. Jesus loved him enough to tell him the truth, which was hidden from him. The truth was that he loved wealth more than he loved God. He did not know this about himself until confronted with the divine command. Jesus's compassion for the rich man was directed to his bondage to wealth, which neither the man nor the society of his day considered a sin. To the contrary, wealth was a blessing and a sign of God's approval. Jesus's demand that the rich man give up his wealth made the man sad. Well, not quite. Jesus's demand revealed the sadness that was already there, and Jesus did not let a false compassion, one focused on subjective feelings, prevent him from seeking the rich man's true welfare and joy.

We must love gay people from a sincere heart that beats in harmony with Jesus's heart. According to the divine truth deposited in Scripture, loving gay people involves telling them the truth even if it makes them sad and angry. Even if they walk away. And the truth is that God made man and woman for each other and same-sex sexual relationships are not part of God's plan for human welfare and happiness. But in telling the truth, we must not forget to look at people and love them. In looking at gay people with Jesus's eyes, we will see in faith the true causes of sadness that are already there and the true reasons for compassion. We should not let false compassion drive us into cruel kindness.

We should not hesitate to interact with gay people. I see a great difference between the Eucharistic table and the common table. It is wrong to partner with a gay-affirming church and participate in the Eucharistic table in a way that affirms gay relationships. It is not wrong to participate at a common table with gay people. In the market place, in the work place, at the gym, and all other secular spaces we should give every person the respect due to God's created image. And if we are able to form friendships with gay people, we should extend hospitality in any way we can. Insofar as we can, we should do good to all people without regard to their moral standing.[36] Let us love in a 1 Corinthians 13 way:

> Love is patient, love is kind. It does not envy, it does not boast, it is not proud. It does not dishonor others, it is not self-seeking, it is not easily angered, it keeps no record of wrongs. Love does not delight in evil but rejoices with the truth. It always protects, always trusts, always hopes, always perseveres. (1 Corinthians 13: 4-7)

Paul, who condemned same-sex intercourse in the strongest terms, also wrote these words:

> Though I am free and belong to no one, I have made myself a slave to everyone, to win as many as possible. To the Jews I became like a Jew, to win the Jews. To those under the law I became like one under the law (though I myself am not under the law), so as to win those under the law. To those not having the law I became like one not having the law (though I am not free from God's law but am

---

[36]One of the most compelling stories I know is of the conversion of Rosaria Champagne Butterfield. A lesbian professor of English literature and an activist in the gay community, she was an unlikely convert indeed. But through the kindness and wisdom of an older pastor and his wife she gradually came to believe and see the need for change. See the account of her conversion in *The Secret Thoughts of an Unlikely Convert: An English Professor's Journey into Christian Faith, Expanded Addition* (Pittsburg: Crown & Covenant Publications, 2014). See also her *The Gospel Comes With a House Key: Practicing Radically Ordinary Hospitality in a Post-Christian World* (Peabody, MA: Crossway, 2018), and *Five Lies of Our Anti-Christian Age* (Peabody, MA: Crossway, 2023).

under Christ's law), so as to win those not having
the law. To the weak I became weak, to win the
weak. I have become all things to all people so that
by all possible means I might save some. I do all
this for the sake of the gospel, that I may share in
its blessings. (1 Corinthians 9:19-23)

Let us follow Paul in accommodating ourselves in
every way consistent with loyalty to Christ to the
weaknesses of others "to win as many as possible." Let
us love gay people the way Jesus loved the rich man.
Let us look at them and love them for their good quali-
ties and feel compassion for their weaknesses. And let
us allow Jesus's love to give us the courage to say, "But
there is one thing you lack...."

Works Cited

Bolz-Weber, Nadia. *Shameless: A Case for Not Feeling Bad About Feeling Good (About Sex).* Reprint edition. Convergent Books, 2020.

Brownson, James V. *Bible, Gender, Sexuality: Reframing the Church's Debate on Same-Sex Relationships.* Grand Rapids: Eerdmans, 2013.

Butterfield, Rosaria Champagne. *The Secret Thoughts of an Unlikely Convert: An English Professor's Journey into Christian Faith, Expanded Addition.* Pittsburg: Crown & Covenant Publications, 2014.

———. *The Gospel Comes With a House Key: Practicing Radically Ordinary Hospitality in a Post-Christian World.* Peabody, MA: Crossway, 2018.

———. *Five Lies of Our Anti-Christian Age.* Peabody, MA: Crossway, 2023.

Campbell, Ted A., Gunter, W. Stephan, et. al. *Wesley and the Quadrilateral: Renewing the Conversation.* Nashville: Abington, 1997.

Gagnon, Robert A. J. *The Bible and Homosexual Practice: Texts and Hermeneutics.* Nashville: Abington, 2002.

Gnuse, Robert K. "Seven Gay Texts: Biblical Passages Used to Condemn Homosexuality." *Biblical Theology Bulletin* 45.2. 2015: 68-87.

Gushee, David P. *After Evangelicalism: The Path to a New Christianity.* Louisville: Westminster John Knox, 2020.

————. *Changing Our Mind: Definitive 3rd Edition of the Landmark Call for Inclusion of LGBTQ Christians with Response to Critics.* Canton, MI: Read the Spirit Books, 2022.

Kaden, David A. *Christianity in Blue: How the Bible, History, Philosophy, and Theology Shape Progressive Christianity.* Minneapolis: Fortress Press, 2021.

Keen, Karen R. *Scripture, Ethics & the Possibility of Same-Sex Relationships.* Grand Rapids: Eerdmans, 2018.

————. *The Word of a Humble God: The Origins, Inspiration, and Interpretation of Scripture.* Grand Rapids: Eerdmans, 2022.

Martin, Colby. *Unclobber: Rethinking our Misuse of the Bible on Homosexuality.* Louisville: Westminster John Knox, 2016.

Olson, Roger. *Against Liberal Theology: Putting the Brakes on Progressive Christianity.* Grand Rapids: Zondervan, 2022.

Peterson, Jeffrey. "The Nuptial Vision of the Bible and its Opponents." *Journal of Christian Studies* 1.2. May 2022: 9-31.

Robertson, Brandan J. *The Gospel of Inclusion: A Christian Case for LGBT+ Inclusion in the Church.* Eugene, OR: Cascade Books, 2022.

Shelly, Rubel. *Male & Female God Made Them: A Biblical Review of LGBTQ+ Claims.* Joplin, MO: College Press, 2023.

————. *The Ink is Dry: God's Distinctive Word on Marriage, Family, and Sexual Responsibility.* Joplin, MO: College Press, 2023.

Vines, Matthew. *God and the Gay Christian.* New York: Convergent Books, 2014.

About the Author

If you feel generous and have a few minutes, please leave a review online where you purchased this book. It makes a significant difference to the author. Thank you in advance.

Ron Highfield (PhD, Rice University) is Professor of Religion at Pepperdine University, Malibu, California. He is the author of *Great is the Lord: Theology for the Praise of God* (Eerdmans, 2008), *God, Freedom & Human Dignity: Embracing a God-Centered Identity in a Me-Centered Culture* (Intervarsity Press, 2013), *The Faithful Creator: Affirming Creation in an Age of Anxiety* (Intervarsity Press, 2015), *The New Adam: What the Early Church Can Teach Evangelicals (and Liberals) About the Atonement* (Cascade, 2021), and a contributor to *Four Views on Divine Providence* (Zondervan, 2011).

Visit the author's website at: http://ifaqtheology.com/ or follow him on Facebook at: http://facebook.com/ron.highfield

About the Publisher

Sulis International Press publishes select fiction and nonfiction in a variety of genres under four imprints:

- Riversong Books (fiction)
- Sulis Press (general nonfiction)
- Keledei Publications (spirituality)
- Sulis Academic Press (academic works)

For more, visit the website at
https://sulisinternational.com

Subscribe to the newsletter at
https://sulisinternational.com/subscribe/

Follow on social media
https://www.facebook.com/SulisInternational
https://twitter.com/Sulis_Intl
https://www.pinterest.com/Sulis_Intl/
https://www.instagram.com/sulis_international/

www.ingramcontent.com/pod-product-compliance
Lightning Source LLC
La Vergne TN
LVHW011334080426
835513LV00006B/343